the Revolt of the Students

Marvin B. Scott

Sonoma State College

Stanford M. Lyman

University of California
at San Diego

Charles E. Merrill Publishing Company
A Bell & Howell Company
Columbus, Ohio

Merrill Social Problems Series

Under the editorship of

Edwin M. Lemert

University of California at Davis

ISBN: 0-675-09303-X

Library of Congress Catalog Card Number: 70-131255

1 2 3 4 5 6 7 8 9 10—79 78 77 76 75 74 73 72 71 70

ACKNOWLEDGMENTS

Excerpts reprinted from *Revolution for the Hell of It* by Abbie Hoffman. Copyright © 1968 by The Dial Press, Inc. and used by permission of the publisher.

From *An Essay on Liberation* by Herbert Marcuse (Boston: Beacon Press, 1969), pp. 25-26, 27-28, and 34-36. Reprinted by permission of the Beacon Press, copyright © 1969 by Herbert Marcuse.

From *Up Against the Ivy Wall* by Jerry L. Alvorn, Robert Friedman, and members of the staff of the Columbia Daily Spectator. Copyright © 1968 by Member of the Board Associates. Reprinted by permission of Atheneum Publishers.

Excerpts reprinted from *Democracy and the Student Left* by George F. Kennan, by permission of Atlantic-Little, Brown and Co. Copyright © 1968 by Little, Brown and Company.

Excerpt from p. 107 of *The City* by Robert E. Park and E.W. Burgess (Chicago: The University of Chicago Press, 1967). Reprinted by permission of The University of Chicago Press.

From "The Case for Separatism: 'Black Perspective'," by Nathan Hare, *Newsweek*, LXXIII (February 10, 1969), 56. Copyright Newsweek, Inc., 1969.

Excerpt from p. 4 of *The New Radicals* by Paul Jacobs and Saul Landau (New York: Vintage Books, 1966). Copyright © 1966 by Random House, Inc. and used by permission of the publisher.

Contents

Chapter I
Introduction

Not long ago the college campus was the heart of pastoral peacefulness, scholastic study, and romantic interludes. Suddenly, it erupted in a kind of open warfare.

Administration and classroom buildings became objects of siege, invasion, and occupation. The stuff of academic life—curricula, documents, and research data—became elements in the struggle. Demands for self-determination, amnesty, and the right to disrupt campus life emerged as standard conditions for settlement. Campuses are now not only places to learn, discover, and love; they are also places for organizing rebellion, launching assaults on selected institutions of the larger society, and restructuring the very nature of college life.

The fundamental feature of student rebellion (or any rebellion, for that matter) may be simply stated: when people become aware of contradictions in the social order—they rebel. But between the awareness of contradictions and the actions that follow lies a vast phenomenological reality. Our efforts will not be to provide a full description of this reality (many separate volumes would be necessary for that task), but to focus on those general elements that must in

1

our view be included in any such description. Our theoretical discussion rests on a body of data gleaned from both a close reading of autobiographical accounts of activists and from our experience as participants in the Berkeley Free Speech Movement (FSM) and the San Francisco State turmoil of 1968–69.

If forced to describe student rebellion in a phrase, we would best refer to it as a "comedy of the absurd." Indeed, our effort in part is to translate this literary allusion into a sociologically intelligible account. Consider first the idea of the "absurd." Translated, this idea initially involves the perception of contradictions in the social order—that is, the awareness of a discrepancy between values and experiences, a condition frequently referred to as *anomie*. When the awareness of anomie is combined with a sense of powerlessness, the world is experienced as *absurd*. Acting in the face of the absurd produces those events that are commonly referred to as rebellion.

The contemporary human comedy finds its dramatic representation in the Theater of the Absurd.[1] And we believe that the disciplined explanation of this human comedy demands a Sociology of the Absurd. Elsewhere we have examined the major analytic elements of such a sociology.[2] Here, it will suffice to note that the task of a Sociology of the Absurd is to show how social actors construct social meaning in the course of action, and through this action transcend absurdity. This task seems to require a game-like model.[3]

The game-theoretic model is especially useful for understanding campus revolts. First, it points up an otherwise overlooked element in these conflicts—fun, and the strategies, tactics, and social re-definitions necessary to create a euphoric atmosphere in an otherwise disagreeable and dangerous situation.[4] Second, it provides an understanding of the modes of behavior in this particular kind of human encounter. In addition to the particular goals sought by students in revolt, other valuable "prizes" are at stake: honor, power, information, and dignity. And each of these will call for actions, orientations, and reprisals that may not be part of the original aim of the movement. Finally, the game-theoretic model calls attention to the peculiar quality of consciousness associated with the revolt. The game framework is a model of behavior of man in consciously problematic situations trying to make sense of, and plans for, that and future situations of a similar nature. This model suggests the contextual establishment of identities, the situation-oriented aliveness to objects and events, and the calculation of strategies. But most important, the game model emphasizes the component of fun. For if the form of drama that best captures the absurdity of the modern world is comedy, then sociological analysis must concentrate on the game-equivalent of comedy—namely, fun. In short, the specific sociological task in examining the phenomenon of absurdity is to describe the sources and functions of fun in games.

Fun, as Erving Goffman has observed,[5] arises out of dual components of the game situation. First, games are fun to play when the outcome is uncertain or the pay-off will remain unsettled until the end of play. The suspense provided by problematic outcomes and the zestful activity of competitors for undetermined pay-offs provide a complex quality of personal feelings and social interaction that is summed up in the term "fun." Second, games provide opportunities to demonstrate qualities and characteristics highly prized in the larger social world, including dexterity, strength, knowledge, intelligence, courage, and self-control. It is the combination of these two principles—problematic outcomes and positively sanctioned displays of character—that produces the emergent quality of fun experienced in game playing.

Now, before we look at the student revolt in game terms, we must first point out that the opportunities for realizing fun are differentially distributed in society. For some, fun is achieved in legitimate sports and games; for others, it is found only in "rumbles," gang fights, and robberies. The commitment to legitimate forms of fun realization is by no means the same for each segment of the population.

For instance, fun for youthful ghetto blacks often takes the form of "kicks." "A 'kick' is any act tabooed by 'squares' that heightens and intensifies the present moment of experience and differentiates it as much as possible from the humdrum routine of daily life."[6] What qualifies an act as a kick is that it have the qualities associated with Huizinga's[7] definition of play: that it be voluntary, unreal, secluded, limited in duration, and aesthetic. Taking drugs, "rolling whitey," sporting the "dandy" costume, and engaging in esoteric sex practices constitute but a few items in the repertoire of the "cat" who is getting his "kicks." And although the dominant ethos may define his life routines as aspects of a shiftless, moribund, and hopeless existence, the "cat seeks through a harmonious combination of charm, ingratiating speech, dress, music, the proper dedication to his 'kick,' and unrestrained generosity to make his day to day life itself a gracious work of art."[8] What constitutes the special humanism of the black ghetto dweller is that he carves out of the interstices of space and opportunity a unique existence, characterized by activities deprecated by the larger society, and verbalized in an innovative argot kept in semi-secrecy from the outside world.[9] Its humanism arises precisely from the fact that in an absurd—that is, meaningless—world, these individual and group-created activities are defined, originated, and controlled by blacks.

Modern youths in general see themselves as victims of a system that invites only compliance, adjustment, and commitment to the socially determined life cycle. If they will postpone their impulses for immediate sexual and hedonistic satisfactions, invest their energies in preparatory education for future careers, align their personalities to indicate not only accordance with but also attachment to the value system in which they find themselves, and enthusiastically accept their fate as pseudo-citizens in a republic benevolently ruled by a military-industrial oligarchy, then they will be rewarded with both the symbols and sureties of the American dream: a comfortable, middle-class existence. Missing from this supposedly sure-fire formula for a pleasant existence is a problematic element, a zestful adventure, a sense of thrilling innovation. Also missing is personal autonomy, individual control of one's destiny, the humanistic element that separates fateful determinism from freedom of choice—in short, what is missing is the opportunity to transcend absurdity.

Individuals who discover their lives to be dominated by forces outside their control often seek to reorient or escape from the determined existence laid out for them. Some young people commit robberies, engage in gang fights, and generally disrupt the community because these acts cause a dramatic shift in their identities from pawns to princes, command the attention of the public, and coerce detection and suppression by the police. These actions are to be expected in a society where youth—in Paul Goodman's fine phrase—grows up absurd.[10]

One response, then, to the anxieties and frustrations of absurdity is the attempt to gamble with fate by attempting to alter the inevitable. An individual might place himself in a particular relationship to an outcome of practical activity, a relationship in which he can attempt to alter the outcome by his own acts, and thus subjectively experience both personal freedom and active mastery. Thus, one manifestation of fate-defying activity is the taking of risks. By flaunting destiny and the directives of history, a man may allow the free play of his own impulses to frustrate ongoing activities, upset the social order, or even wreak havoc on society. Persons who openly violate the rules of tact and propriety at social occasions are an example of the first; the reckless driving of a car at top speed through a slow-moving funeral cortege exemplifies the second; and the spirited ideologist who is sure that the forces of history have chosen him to strike the fatal blow to the present society illustrates the last. Although these activities are often defined by others as deviant, they may be viewed from quite another perspective as acts that transcend absurdity by producing a sense of "courageous" humanism. The man who rudely challenges the honor of his host at a cocktail party forces recognition of his heretofore unrecognized capacities, for his remarks cause others to respond. The rude guest becomes the cause for others to act, and thus he converts his identity from object to subject, from billiard ball to pool cue. In the same way, the reckless driver demands capture by the police, and the revolutionary dictates that counter-insurgent measures be taken against him. Coping with absurdity involves this dialectical sequence of solving troubles and causing them. Bold acts, then, are usually infractions—against the laws, social norms, or personal propriety—that invite counteractions.[11] It is the realization that he has caused another to act, forced a response, and created the conditions of counteraction that gives the "little man" just that evidence to assure him that, at least for the moment, he controls destiny.

Risky acts plunge those who undertake them into an episode of adventure. Adventures have as one of their unique qualities the capacity to relocate individuals with respect to time and fate. The adventure is separated in an almost absolute sense from linear time and interconnected events. It is, as Simmel has observed, "independent of the 'before' and 'after'; its boundaries are defined regardless of them."[12] Because of the fundamental disconnectedness, because of its existence in time and space *sui generis*, the adventure offers relief and rehabilitation to those who sense that their lives are ruled by uncontrollable destiny. For its duration, the individual is freed from the dictates of time and subject only to his voluntary acts or to that which befalls him within the scope of the chosen enterprise—and he is re-created as master of the scene. Adventures are the stuff from which "heroes" emerge; they offer just those opportunities to employ wit and skill that fate had otherwise foreclosed.

Most adventures are of a limited duration. Unlike the whole of the life cycle, or the lengthy period required to develop a career, the adventure collapses the scene of realizable action into a single episode, or into a stacatto-like series of episodes. The man who bets his life savings on a horse, the husband who boldly carries on an assignation while his wife is in another room, the student who gives up his baccalaureate year to strike against the university—in each case, he realizes the outcome of his actions in a very short time. The bettor may have a turn of luck which in a few moments may end his financial worries for all time; the husband may experience new sensuous pleasures and affectionate responses that have been denied to him for all of his married life; and the student may win laurels in the few days of the strike that would never have been his in all the years of his degree-guaranteed career.

The adventure also requires a peculiar combination of chance and rationality not found in the same corelationship in everyday life. Thus, when students decide on a moment's notice to refuse to vacate an occupied building, to resist policemen attempting to arrest them, and to wait out the terrifying confrontation that will inevitably ensue, they pit their skills and hopes on outcomes that are by no means assured. Moreover, their single though complex decision not to leave the building peaceably as ordered has consequences beyond the episodic outcome of the particular situation.[13] The students may be arrested and convicted of a crime, expelled from college, and forced to define their life situations in ways quite different from those that preceded the risky decision. Thus, the adventurous gamble may be more than a temporary interruption of an ongoing life style. It may terminate that life-style entirely. The brilliant Ph.D. candidate in physics may be forced to eke out his living as a bartender after he is expelled for participation in a student strike; the talented but modest and shy undergraduate may be propelled into a career of street-corner demagoguery after his first fiery speech introduces a heretofore unrecognized charisma; the virginity of the coed who publicly denounces the puritanical standards of the university may be the first sacrifice in the proof of her own convictions. But at the moment of the decision, none of these outcomes is assured; the situation is wholly problematical. Like Machiavelli's Prince, the adventurous student must strike out without knowing exactly what awaits him, measuring his capacities against what fate has to offer. The proper mood for such a move is one of euphoric optimism; the proper experience during the course of the adventure is, above all, exhilaration; the proper orientation toward the whole enterprise is one that views it with the spirit of a long-desired humanism: the adventure offers one the opportunity to express the unfettered self, and in the process, to transcend absurdity.[14]

Although much of the content of campus revolt is experienced as fun-filled adventure, fun is not the only causal component of behavior that operates in the decision to enter into such a revolt. The behavioral conditions conducive to the commission of infractions in general are operative in the decision to enter into and to continue to carry out campus revolts in particular. It will be useful here to consider them under the headings of preparation, apprehension, and desperation.[15]

By preparation, we mean learning through experience that something regarded as an infraction *can be* done, a technical precondition to the moral holiday that will be declared when it *will be* done. Now, the specific activities that are connected with campus revolts require little more than the ordinary abilities possessed by every man. Drawing posters, carrying signs, making sandwiches, sleeping on hard floors, are quite ordinary activities associated with situations that are lawful and commonplace.

If the particular technical aspects of campus revolution do not require any unusual new learning, the total gestalt of their commission, the commencement of an action taken in violation of rules or law, does call for a special orientation to overcome the fear and shame that are usually deterrents to infractions. Apprehensions may prevent someone from entering into a revolt, not because he is physically incapable of carrying out the appropriate acts, but because he is unable to manage his own general fears, or to neutralize his knowledge of the consequences of the act to be committed. Those who do join a revolt find some way to overcome their vague but powerful qualms and to discount the consequences.

One way to reduce apprehension is to emphasize the impotence and incompetence of the authorities one challenges. The redesignation of police as "pigs," university administrators as "uptight honkies," and the society as a whole as "sick," detracts from their authority and power. Coupled with the students' own emphasis on their youth, enthusiasm, potency, and righteousness, this double-barreled argument helps to lessen fears and thus to counteract the deterrent elements of the situation.

A second way to manage their apprehensiveness is to discount the consequences that arise from their acts. Universities and colleges typically have some mode of graded punishments for infraction. But these sanctions were devised for use in instances of individual violation, not for mass acts. Even so, these sanctions are ambiguous, trivial, or rather easily circumvented. The same prohibited act may often be committed many times with impunity or rather light punishment. Furthermore, some of the acts that are presently part of college revolt—such as sit-ins, mass demonstrations, and occupation of buildings—were not countenanced by the original rules on campus conduct. Finally, relief from any punishment—the insistence on amnesty—is usually one of the demands that students make at the very moment of their revolt. Thus, the negative consequences that could arise from the disturbances on campus are either unclear in the first instance, sufficiently inconsequential to deter violations, or subject to reduction or complete negation by negotiation and bargaining.

The will to join the campus revolt, however, is not triggered simply by reducing fears and discounting sanctions. Campus revolts are hazardous, and there are, in addition to the known and fearsome consequences of such participation, those vague, amorphous, and terrifying unknowns —about self and future—that arise to plague young people caught up in today's college atmosphere. In such a situation students feel they are at sea, drifting somewhere between the safe shore of conformity and the dangerous but salubrious bank of liberation from society's dictates. Whether they move closer to one or the other shore is a function of how desperate they feel. And desperation is heightened by the mood of fatalism that prevails in greater or lesser degrees among young people in America.

Fatalism "refers to the experience of seeing one's self as effect,"[16] that is, the feeling that one is neither in control of his environment nor the master of his future. The mood of fatalism receives ideational support from the belief that American society is in fact a creature of the industrial corporations, military planners, and political insiders who make all the important decisions. A special sense of fatalism is suggested by black and other racial minorities who argue that their lives and futures are dominated by the vague but seemingly invincible white power structure.

The general mood of fatalism is usually insufficient to move people to engage in humanistic, control-restoring action. Such action usually requires the specific and personal sense of being "pushed around," of having lost active mastery of the situation. School administrators encourage such a feeling when they indicate in no uncertain terms that students do not count. Thus, when the provost at Columbia University said, "Whether students vote 'yes' or 'no' on a given issue means as much to me as if they were to tell me they like strawberries,"[17] he brought home to many students at that university just how much their vote—presumably an instrument of control in a democratic institution —meant. For many students the administration's invalidation of a student election, the college president's "freeze" on the spending of student body funds, and the frustrating, cumbersome, and paternalistic rules that are characteristic of campus codes of conduct generate a desperate search for autonomy. And for many more, the presence of police on campus, the arbitrary prohibition or brutal breakup of protests and demonstrations, and the violent suppression of student revolts, remind them of their lack of freedom and loss of personal and social mastery.

Indeed, the sense of desperation that motivates people to strike out in an act of humanistic liberation is often a collective, psycho-social goal of early activist tactics, a move to trigger a desperate mass response to a collective mood of fatalism that, until the particular tactic is carried out, was sensed by but a few. Thus Mark Rudd spoke of the functions of confrontation politics for "radicalizing" the individual:

> Confrontation politics . . . forces [the enemy] to define himself. In addition, it puts the individual up against the wall. He has to make a choice. Radicalization of the individual means that he must commit himself to the struggle to change society as well as share the radical view of what is wrong with society.[18]

Once desperation is sufficiently sensed, once the mood of fatalism becomes too constricting to bear, the will to commit infractions that will, by their very nature, invite counteraction, is activated. Infractions—in the case of the campus revolt, violations of university codes and public laws—provide a dramatic assurance that one can make things happen, that one is still capable of command—in sum, a jolting but autonomous restoration of one's own active mastery, of personal control, of one's humanism.

The behavioral conception of preparation, apprehension, and desperation takes us part of the way toward our understanding of the impetus for a student revolt. However, just as significant in shaping the outcome of revolt-generating situations is the societal reaction.

The fate of any social movement depends on societal reactions. Especially important are the official agencies of social control[19]—police, courts, legislators, administrators—whose interpretations of and counteractions to the inchoate beliefs and amorphous actions of protesters crystallize these phenomena, giving them both name and form. Indeed, the importance of societal reaction to student activists has been recognized by some protest leaders themselves, so that tactics and strategy are organized around a game-like assessment of just what kinds of counteraction are likely to follow from an initial action. Thus, if a small but vociferous group of activists wishes to create a mass following of students, one tactic would be to harass the administration by just the amount of nonviolent disruption (sit-ins, demonstrations, protest marches) that will invite a cruel and violent counteraction. Those students who are ambivalent, and those who, until the counteraction, had stood by in silent sympathy, unwilling to join in because the issues had not been sufficiently critical to move them to action, might then join in the struggle, galvanized into action not by the original issue, but rather by the over-reaction to it.

The game quality of this group interaction is much like that in chess, courtship, or war. The "opponents"—in the case of student revolts, this includes administrators, police, and legislators—may sense that they are involved in a situation in which one side is actively and consciously employing strategy and tactics. Once they sense this, they too will begin to think strategically, try to dope out the *real* meaning of the students' actions, and figure out just what counter-strategy would thwart their aims.[20]

One problem that arises here is that of assessing priorities. What is the real ultimate aim of the protest? Is it to end ROTC on the campus as *some* student leaflets say, or is that just a cover for a more encompassing objective: the radicalizing of the campus, the creation of polarized factions, and the beginning of a fundamental revolution? The college administrator, the faculty, and the police are frequently faced with the nearly impossible task of sorting out means and ends in student protest and assessing information to distinguish one from the other. The assessment is made even more difficult by the strategic use that may be made of information itself. Thus, for example, students who really wish to end ROTC on campus might give the impression that they seek much wider and more earth-shattering goals, to make their actual objective appear as a minor concession which the administration might offer to conciliate them. Or, to the contrary, students might play up their specific demands, pointing to their moderateness, facility of expedition, and general value, while simultaneously acting in such a manner as to invite a repressive counter-measure whose consequence turns out to be their real (but secret) goal: the polarization of the campus into irreconcilable factions.

This rational assessment of actual goals is further complicated by the phenomenon of ideological amorphousness among the students. Although it is asserted in some circles that the current revolts are the product of a conspiracy, the evidence suggests that something far more complex is afoot. There are ideologists of various persuasions among the students, and some of these are indeed group leaders, but the existence of ideologists and leadership in *groups* does not explain a *mass* following. What is unknown in any instant campus revolt, what perhaps never can be known fully, is the meaning attached to that situation by the followers—that body of nameless soldiers who lay life and future on the line for something which means that much to them. The information game that is strategically played by the *leaders* on both sides of an insurrectionary movement must somehow grapple with the next-to-impossible task of discovering the definition of the situation of their own and their opponent's followers. This is also a task for the sociologist.

It seems crucial, then, to attempt to uncover the origin and nature of the conceptual frame in terms of which the mass of students are constructing their world. By conceptual frame is meant ideology. Thus, in Chapter Two, we will depict the major features of mass society as the sources of the student ideology. We will suggest which elements of mass society have generated the perception of anomic social contradictions. These contradictions constitute the felt disturbance with which the ideology attempts to cope. In Chapter Three, we will discuss the nature of the ideology of student rebellion that legitimates the actions undertaken in its name. We will also note in Chapter Three the close connection between the perceived social contradictions of mass society and the specific content of the ideology. In Chapter Four, we will examine more closely the mechanisms that facilitate the persistence of the ideology and the sources of fun that also feedback to reaffirm a belief in the principles of the ideology. Finally, in Chapter Five, we will offer two independent though related interpretations of student revolution that highlight both its agony and its ecstasy.

Notes

[1] See Martin Esslin, *Theater of the Absurd* (Garden City: Doubleday Anchor, 1961).

[2] Stanford M. Lyman and Marvin B. Scott, *A Sociology of the Absurd* (New York: Appleton-Century-Crofts, 1970).

[3] We have explored this approach analytically in our essay, "Game Frameworks," in *A Sociology of the Absurd, ibid.*

[4] See Erving Goffman, "Fun in Games," *Encounters* (Indianapolis: Bobbs-Merrill, 1961), pp. 17-84.

[5] *Ibid.*, pp. 67-68.

[6] Harold Finestone, "Cats, Kicks, and Color," *Social Problems*, V (July, 1957), 5. Our discussion here is informed by this essay.

[7] Johan Huizinga, *Homo Ludens* (Boston: Beacon Press, 1955).

[8] Finestone, *op. cit.*, p. 5.

[9] For a psycholinguistic analysis of Negro argot, see Roger D. Abrahams, *Deep Down in the Jungle* (Hatboro, Penn.: Folklore Associates, 1964).

[10] Paul Goodman, *Growing Up Absurd* (New York: Vintage, 1962).

[11] David Matza, *Delinquency and Drift* (New York: John Wiley, 1964), pp. 182-91.

[12] Georg Simmel, "The Adventure," in *Georg Simmel, 1858-1918*, ed. Kurt H. Wolff (Columbus, Ohio: Ohio State University Press, 1959), p. 244.

[13] See Erving Goffman, "Where the Action Is," *Interaction Ritual* (Garden City: Doubleday Anchor, 1968), pp. 156-61.

[14] See the brilliant essay by Maurice Merleau-Ponty, "A Note on Machiavelli," in *Signs*, trans. Richard C. McCleary (Evanston, Ill.: Northwestern University Press, 1964), pp. 211-23.

[15] Here we follow David Matza, *op. cit.*, pp. 181-91.

[16] *Ibid.*, p. 188.

[17]Jerry L. Alvorn, ed., *Up Against the Ivy Wall* (New York: Atheneum, 1968), p. 119.

[18]*Ibid.*, p. 33.

[19]On this point see especially Neil Smelser, *Theory of Collective Behavior* (New York: Free Press of Glencoe, 1963); see also Edwin M. Lemert, "The Concept of Secondary Deviation," in *Human Deviance, Social Problems, and Social Control* (Englewood Cliffs, N.J.: Prentice-Hall, 1967), pp. 40-64.

[20]The theoretical points underlying the analysis here are found in Erving Goffman's unpublished manuscript, "Strategic Interaction and Communication." For a further application of Goffman's points, see Marvin B. Scott, *The Racing Game* (Chicago: Aldine Press, 1968), especially pp. 158-70.

Chapter II

Mass Society and the Ideology of Rebellion

Student rebellion and its ideology can be understood only in terms of the context in which they occur. That context is mass society.

The characteristics, and especially the negative features, of mass society have been described or decried by all classical sociologists. Max Weber, for instance, called painful attention to the inertia of highly developed capitalist societies, which had begun with an adventurous spirit and the dreadful fascination with man's fate, but had evolved into the ritualistic routine, deadening drudgery, and dutiful detail of man's fatalism:

> The Puritan wanted to work in a calling; we are forced to do so. For when asceticism was carried out of monastic cells into everyday life, and began to dominate worldly morality, it did its part in building the tremendous cosmos of the modern economic order. This order is now bound to the technical and economic conditions of machine production which today determine the lives of all individuals who are born into this mechanism, not only those directly concerned with economic acquisition, with irresistible force. Perhaps it will so determine them until the last ton of fossilized

coal is burst. In Baxter's view the care for external goods should only be on the shoulders of the "saint like a light cloak, which can be thrown aside at any moment." But fate decreed that the cloak should become an iron cage. . . .

No one knows who will live in this cage in the future, or whether at the end of this tremendous development entirely new prophets will arise, or there will be a great rebirth of old ideas and ideals, or, if neither, mechanized petrification, embellished with a sort of convulsive self-importance. For of the last stage of this cultural development, it might well be truly said: "Specialists without spirit, sensualists without heart; this nullity imagines that it has attained a level of civilization never before achieved."[1]

Stripped of an animating *raison d'etre*, estranged from his fellow men by the interposition of specialized functions and tasks, and imprisoned in the routinized workaday activities of industrial existence, man came more and more to depend on the ever-fleeting possibilities of the inno-vative, the exciting and the eudaemonic. And—according to theorists of mass society—under the impact of these new possibilities, there resulted both the loss of authority and the loss of community.

The loss of authority finds its most manifest form in the delegitima-tion of all traditional and legal elites in the name of the legitimation by the masses of themselves.[2] The loss of community becomes clear when men can no longer count on common interests deriving among themselves on the bases of blood, caste, or condition.[3] It reaches its penultimate state when they sense a dreaded isolation from their com-monly constituted peers, and it reaches its apotheosis when man feels his total estrangement from himself as well.[4] From these twin phe-nomena—the decline of authority and community—there follows a decline in moral consensus and a great readiness for mobilization on the part of the masses.[5] The disappearance of moral consensus makes life less predictable than it has been before and insures that everyday man may be confronted by puzzles, crises, and incomprehensible wonders at any moment. The vulnerability to mobilization guarantees that social life will be characterized by vicissitudes of numbing voids followed by exhilarating crazes, fads, and excitements. The idea of conformity en-shrouds man's behavior, but this conformity is constantly interrupted and violated by sudden surprises, deviant characters, and outrageous acts.[6]

American society has increasingly become just such a mass society. The developments along this path have been noted by sociologists, sometimes with a despairing cry coupled with the tragic sense that they were witnessing the historically inevitable. Thus, more than forty years ago, Robert E. Park saw in the rise of juvenile delinquency in America a much deeper and more pervasive malaise, affecting not just the adolescent but the whole of society:

> We are living in . . . a period of individualization and social disorganization. Everything is in a state of agitation—everything seems to be undergoing a change. Society is, apparently, not much more than a congeries of social atoms. Habits can be formed only in a relatively stable environment, even if that stability consists merely—as, in fact, it invariably does, since there is nothing in the universe that is absolutely static—in a relatively constant form of change. Any form of change that brings any measurable alteration in the routine of social life tends to break up habits; and in breaking up the habits upon which the existing social organization rests, destroys that organization itself.[7]

But, as Park noted, the rapid pace and merciless operation of impersonal forces resulted in both a significantly large accumulation of human wreckage and a passionate desire for hedonistic escape. "Our great cities," he wrote, "are full of junk, much of it human, i.e., men and women who, for some reason or other, have fallen out of line in the march of industrial progress and have been scrapped by the industrial organization of which they were once a part."[8] For those not left beside the track of industrial development, however, life consists of an insistent busyness, of work that makes men lose sight altogether of the communities in which they live. And in those moments when he is freed from work, modern man vainly seeks after a will-o'-the-wisp hedonism to counteract the emptiness of life:

> Our leisure is now mainly a restless search for excitement. It is the romantic impulse, the desire to escape the dull routine of life at home and in the local community, that drives us abroad in search of adventure. This romantic quest, which finds its most outrageous expression in the dance halls and jazz parlors, is characteristic of almost every other expression of modern life.[9]

Park went on to assert that the contrast between manifestly boring work and potentially exhilarating leisure explained not only the fads, crazes and fantasies so prevalent today, but the political and millenial religious movements as well. "Political revolution and social reform are themselves often merely expressions of this same romantic impulse," he wrote. "Millenialism in religion, the missionary enterprises, particularly those that are limited to 'regions beyond,' are manifestations of this same wish to escape reality."[10]

Whether in the form of romantic fantasies, chiliastic religion, absorption in gadgetry, or the spinning of utopian societies, modern man is forever seeking to escape from the round of life imposed on him by technological progress and conformist social order.

Conditions
of Mass
Society

Daniel Bell has provided a capsule statement of the nature of mass society which, despite his own critique, admirably describes it:

> The revolutions in transport and communications have brought men into closer contact with each other and bound them in new ways; the division of labor has made them more interdependent; tremors in one part of society affect all others. Despite this greater interdependence, however, individuals have grown more estranged from one another. The old primary group ties of family and local community have been shattered; ancient parochial faiths are questioned; few unifying values have taken their place. Most important, the critical standards of an educated elite no longer shape opinion or taste. As a result, mores and morals are in constant flux, relations between individuals are tangential or compartmentalized, rather than organic. At the same time, greater mobility, spatial and social, intensifies concern over status. Instead of a fixed or known status, symbolized by dress or title, each person assumes a multiplicity of roles and constantly has to prove himself in a succession of new situations. Because of all this, the individual loses a coherent sense of self. His anxieties increase. There ensues a search for new faiths. The stage is thus set for the charismatic leader, the secular messiah, who, by bestowing upon each person the semblance of necessary grace and of fullness of personality, supplies a substitute for the older unifying belief that the mass society has destroyed.[11]

Bell's statement summarizes the thesis that has developed over the centuries about mass society and its miseries. Critics of the thesis have quibbled over the ambiguous employment of the word "mass,"[12] or have argued (incorrectly, as Kornhauser[13] has shown) that mass society is the social construct of those who hark back to the alleged joys of a primitive society or to the theological consensus of an aristocratic one.[14] We do not intend, however, to enter into this debate. The passage of events has made it irrelevant to debate the logical consistency of the term "mass" or to isolate the "real" political motives or nostalgic biases of those who lament the coming of mass society. For today, mass society as it has been envisioned by philosophers and sociologists finds its expression in the social construction of reality given by students in revolt.

The language once employed only by scholars and intellectuals to describe modern society *is now part of everyday speech*. Students and their compatriots speak voluably of their own alienation, atomization, dull conformity, and rootless homogeneity. Some develop a passionate attachment to a particular cause; others devote themselves to the revolution that will utterly transform society and liberate its slaves; still others have sunk into a pathos of disillusionment and demoralization that resembles nothing so much as Freud's description of melancholia: "a profoundly painful dejection, abrogation of interest in the outside world, loss of the capacity to love, inhibition of all activity, and a lowering of the self-regarding feelings to a degree that finds utterances in self-reproaches and self-revilings, and culminates in a delusional expectation of punishment."[15] (Indeed, the latter two characteristics find institutional representation in the "encounter groups" formed by some of the "modern" young people, groups that have as one of their activities the mutual chastisement of their members, followed by remorseful confessions, and reconceptualizations of self.) Our point, then, is that mass society—no matter how illogical its formulation, no matter how primitive or aristocratic its nostalgic leanings—is part of the commonsensical understanding of the everyday world by a significant segment of the population, and that there is an elective affinity between the "theory" of mass society and the student revolt.

We turn now to three of the salient conditions characteristic of mass society. Our emphasis will be on the elective affinity of these conditions for the ideology of student revolt. These conditions are (1) pluralism of interests, castes, classes, and groups under conditions of physical concentration; (2) impersonality, anonymity, and freedom; and (3) social and geographic mobility.

Pluralism[16]

Pluralistic society suggests the existence of a multiplicity of identities and meanings and a context of situated moralities wherein universal rules of ethics are less, if at all, relevant. Pluralism may entail differences among status groups and persons such that special languages and peculiar argot are employed, objects and individuals do not enjoy common identification, variations exist in agreement on acceptable and prohibited behavior, and no common hierarchy of values can be discovered. If the pluralistic elements of the society rub shoulders with one another—a feature more likely because modern societies require task interdependence at the same time that they encourage multiple group formations— there is an extreme likelihood of misunderstandings, violations, and a great variety of other social mishaps. Under situations of value consensus, of what W. I. Thomas called a common "apperception mass," excuses and justifications might mend the social fabric, throw bridges over the breaches in social relations, and smooth over the cracks in the cake of customary solidarity.[17] When, however, value consensus cannot be presumed, then there can be no presumption that any rhetoric of motives and exculpation will suffice to repair the breaks occasioned by contacts among heterogeneous peoples.

Recognition of the multiple values in a pluralistic society is but one element of its understanding. Another is the nature and scope of legitimate power in the society. The several groups that make up a plural society do not possess equal power or authority. Indeed, in most societies, plural or not, we can speak of one or several power elites who possess certain rights over others and who, usually, give legitimate expression to a specific value pattern and morality. Because of their authority, the value pattern and moral beliefs of the power elites tend to take precedence over all other value structures and moralities, at least in the mass media, and in all those situations in which individuals and groups come into contact with, and must acknowledge at least formal acquiescence to, the authority of power holders. In the latter situations, there is not only a potentiality for confusion in communication and contradiction in morality, but also the hazard of pain and deprivation resulting from a failure to indicate agreement with the moral values of the power holders.

Typically, in multi-group societies, certain functionaries act as agents of and representatives for persons or groups who find themselves outside the pale of legitimated morality or at odds with the law. In modern societies this task usually falls to the attorney—although clergymen, professors, and psychiatrists sometimes act in this capacity. These functionaries often find that their principal and most difficult task is to legitimate the excuses and justifications given for untoward acts committed by persons untutored in, or out of sorts with, prevailing moral beliefs or legal requirements. Such legitimation is made easier when the offending parties are willing to have their prohibited deeds excused or justified on grounds which, while not conforming to their own views, are efficacious in reducing punishment or avoiding blame. However, when the accused parties insist not only on the right to commit the proscribed acts but also on the right to justify these acts on "private" grounds, then the limits of pluralistic toleration are quickly reached. As one astute observer has pointed out,[18] ideologues of pluralism have usually insisted on just that amount of sub-societal variation to preserve separate cultural traditions, but not so much as to make community cooperation difficult or joint civic actions impossible. But once pluralistic developments are occurring, there is no insurance that they will not pass beyond this point of societal toleration.

If the several solidarities comprising pluralistic societies are maintained in a state of "communalism,"[19]—that is, their social organization is such that disparate groups coexist under a common authority but at great cultural distance—then the problems of value and norm differences may be reduced to a minimum. For example, under the colonial method known as indirect rule, tribes, nations, races, and ethnic groups paid common homage to a distant Occidental authority while exercising considerable local control over their own social, economic, cultural, and hedonistic activities.[20] Segregation from other culture groups and the appointment of headmen from among their own ranks maintained cultural tradition and reduced intercultural contacts. The plural society under colonialism operated with a minimum of conflict when both the supreme authority and the local communities felt they were maximizing their interests.

Such perfect cultural separation, however, is nearly impossible to bring about in modern societies because of the coexistence within them of independent cultural, economic, and interest groups, and interdependent tasks and social relationships.[21] Making a living, getting an education, enjoying leisure, and seeking or dispensing services provide just those situations wherein peoples meet.[22] When a society allows immigration from culturally different countries, it opens itself up to interethnic contacts and, on occasion, conflicts as well. Moreover, even when portions of that society, once culturally distinct, have come to share a common outlook, they are still subject to division in interests, debates over methods, and destruction by innovative ideologies, not to mention their disparate perspectives on or desperate responses to the demands of the as yet unacculturated people inhabiting the country.[23]

It is in these contacts that cross social and cultural lines that persons are likely to violate one another's expectations, shock one another's consciences, and bring themselves into potential or actual conflict.

When, for example, a portion of America's youth publicly and voluntarily renounces the use of almost all those external symbols and artifices of bourgeois life, and adopt instead the demeanor of bohemians, the habits of mendicants, the hygienic practices of hoboes, and the habituations of hermits, and when they do this not in the pastoral seclusion of a sequestered monastery but rather in the workaday presence of the ordinary urbanite, they are likely not only to be called to account for their strange behavior, but to be challenged by public authorities as well.

Less dramatically, but no less poignantly, the encounters between individuals sharing different perspectives on life and values are fraught with the possibilities of misunderstandings and conflict. Even the excuses and justifications that are believed to be commonly understood may not suffice in such encounters. Professors may be astonished to learn that their black students expect to employ the special argot and rhetorical flourishes of the urban ghetto in their academic dialogue. Businessmen may discover to their outrage that prospective employees appear for their interviews in the dress once found only in the slums, bohemia, or the theater. Men may be chagrined to learn that some women not only disparage them for their middle-class chivalric etiquette, but also expect equal treatment on all occasions—occupational, social and personal.

Finally, modern plural societies are not typically static. Two dimensions of their dynamics are relevant here. First, as we have already mentioned, their interdependency is likely to throw together persons of distinct and disparate social, cultural and political backgrounds, create situations of unavoidable engagement between persons having mutually offensive habits, and engender irregular but frequent encounters among those who are not like-minded. Second, their tendency for social change and cultural reconstruction insures that no mode of stratification will be sufficiently permanent to freeze social relations into an unchangeable system. Plural societies in the contemporary era consist not only of the relatively autonomous subsystems of race, class, occupation and clique, but also of shifts in power and status relationships among these groups. Unlike the Estates of France during the *Ancien Regime*, anyone of the several groups in modern society might now hold a less favorable but later hold a more favorable position. In such a fluid system, norms are unstable and behavior patterns unpredictable. Identities fluctuate and individuals are constantly forced to face the puzzling question: Who am I?

To summarize our analysis: modern societies are characterized by a complex pluralism. When there is a proliferation of social solidarities, when status groups are mobile, contacts between discrepant social types frequent, and the legitimacy of the power elite questionable, social order is problematic and personal identities insecure. In such a society there is a highly fragmented and precarious consensus, a bewilderment of meanings, and a deep sense of frustration in the enforcement of obligations.

Impersonality, Anonymity,
and Freedom

The familiar societal dichotomies in sociology—status-contract, Gemeinschaft-Gesellschaft, sacred-secular, primary-secondary, community-society, folk-urban—call attention to the impersonality of modern societies. Whether regarded as historical change or heuristic device, these sets of terms highlight a transformation in social relations which emphasizes impersonality, social distance, and personal inhibition.

Technological developments and institutional specificity have made roles a basic part of man's existence. The social relationship described by this term implies the separation of the cognitive from the affective self and the inhibition of the latter.[24] Although the term "role" is frequently used to describe the patterned behavior of any status, here we wish to restrict the term to patterns of behavior that arise from the normative constraint on affective spontaneity. Impersonality is the general characteristic of social relationships based upon exchange of commodities or services among strangers. And modern society is best described as a social organization of interdependent strangers. Hence it follows that in public life men must conduct themselves in accordance with certain mutually patterned expectations: universality of outlook, rational calculation of gains and losses, and the relative surety that extraordinary affections and griefs, outbursts and displays, effusions and romances, will not modify contractual agreements.

Social distance is the concomitant of a public life organized around the idea of contract. It is precisely because men are ordinarily so spatially proximate in their negotiations everywhere, so constantly in seemingly familiar association and usually so regularly engaged in transactions of limited purpose, that their relationships are vulnerable to improvident importunities. The rhetorical styles appropriate to impersonal relationships are consultative and formal.[25] As a result, friendship is both deemphasized and debased. As Talcott Parsons has well observed, "Among men it tends rather to be attached . . . to occupational relationships in the form of an obligation in a mild way to treat one's occupational associate as a friend also."[26] And, as some modern dramatists[27] and psychoanalysts have noted, the loss of affection, especially if it is "overvalued"—a condition perhaps likely in just those societies wherein it is officially regarded as nonutilitarian and as an impediment—is likely to result in a pervasive and gnawing sense of despair.[28]

Individuals in modern mass industrial societies are likely to experience life as if it had some of the properties of a theatrical drama. People seem to feel called upon to present themselves in everyday life in accordance with performance expectations thrust upon them by rules, roles, and rituals, and in accordance with some calculation of the meaning and consequences of situations.[29] This sense of leading life on a stage is, of course, not experienced to the same poignant degree by all members of society. In its most general sense, fears and anxieties and a consciousness of having to present oneself—rather than just be oneself—arise whenever situations are perceived as having consequential risks for the interactants.[30] For many people, the consciousness of having to perform, rather than to be, arises only occasionally; for some it occurs more frequently; for others it haunts the consciousness, challenging an inner sense of self that feels imprisoned behind the façade of the personal; and for a few—those who must hide their real identity because its discovery would lead to shame or discredit—the sense of always being an actor, of constantly conspiring in a deception, of participating in everyday life in bad faith, is ubiquitous.[31]

The sense of personal inhibition and enforced theatricality that arises out of man's apparent necessity to play roles was recognized by Robert E. Park as both a condition of human existence and a cause for personal distress.[32] "It is probably no mere historical accident . . . that the word 'person,' in its first meaning, is a mask. It is rather a recognition of the fact that everyone is always and everywhere, more or less consciously, playing a role. We are parents and children, masters and servants, teachers and students, clients and professional men, Gentiles and Jews. It is in these roles that we know each other; it is in these roles that we know ourselves." Man's acts and their meanings are carried on socially, however, and as a result, "the individual in society lives a more or less public existence, in which all his acts are anticipated, checked, inhibited, or modified by the gestures and the intentions of his fellows." The social conflict that arises among men is concerned in part with the sense of distrust that prevails when persons confront one another in their respective roles. "In any case, it is an effort for any of us to maintain the attitudes which we assume; all the more difficult when the world refuses to take us at our own estimates of ourselves. Being actors, we are consciously or unconsciously seeking recognition, and failure to win it is, at the very least, a depressing, often a heartbreaking, experience." When men are anxious over the acceptability of their identities, concerned over their ability to bring off a desired presentation, or apprehensive about their role performances, they are likely to suffer from stage fright and to experience many of the agonies that are regular features of a dramatic actor's life.[33]

But role performance also produces a conflict within the individual. It is not only that he experiences a sense of unreality, bad faith, or inadequacy in his role performances before others, but also that he feels imprisoned within these roles, unable to break out of them and live according to his spontaneous desires. Park writes:

> We have a private and a public life. In seeking to live up to the role which we have assumed, and which society has imposed upon us, we find ourselves in a constant conflict with ourselves. Instead of acting simply and naturally, as a child, responding to each natural impulse as it arises, we seek to conform to accepted models, and conceive ourselves in some one of the conventional and socially accepted patterns. In our efforts to conform, we restrain our immediate and spontaneous impulses, and act, not as we are impelled to act, but rather as seems appropriate and proper to the occasion.

In engaging in this restraint, individuals acquire a character that fits like a mask, hiding their own true feelings from others, and also, inevitably, hiding them from themselves. "Our very faces are living masks," Park asserts, "which reflect, to be sure, the changing emotions of our inner lives but which more and more tend to conform to the type we are seeking to impersonate." Finally, despite our frustrations over it, the mask may come to represent the truer self, the self with which we identify or the self in which we should like to appear. "So, at any rate, our mask becomes at last an integral part of our personality; becomes second nature. We come into the world as individuals, achieve character, and become persons." But as persons, we nostalgically wish to resume our identity as individuals, despairingly resent our requirement to live in accordance with roles, and—at least some of us—muse on the possibilities of restructuring the world so that individuality may remove our masks forever.

Social Mobility

With the important exception of certain racial minorities and pockets of poor whites, the American people have experienced a remarkable amount of upward mobility, so that for them there has been a reasonable and fortunate relationship between the promise of American society and the performance of its institutions.[34] But the absorption over the years of significant numbers of Americans into the middle class has not been an unalloyed success story; rather, it has been accompanied by status anxieties arising out of the dilemmas imposed by a society dedicated simultaneously to equalitarianism and achievement.

Precisely because American society lacks a feudal past and an aristocratic present—that is, because no fixed and unalterable statuses, with their attendant symbols, exist in America—those who rise in the social order find themselves surrounded by others who resemble them in every way. The problem of the upwardly mobile is to make their mobility somehow visible. More than a century ago, Alexis de Tocqueville observed the state of restless anxiety among Americans and attributed it in part to the unanticipated consequences of rapid upward mobility within the framework of an ethic of equality. Tocqueville's words are worth quoting at length:

> It is odd to watch with what feverish ardor the Americans pursue prosperity and how they are ever tormented by the shadowy suspicion that they may not have chosen the shortest route to get it.
>
> Americans cleave to the things of this world as if assured that they will never die, and yet are in such a rush to snatch any that come within their reach, as if expecting to stop living before they have relished them. They clutch everything but hold nothing fast, and so lose grip as they hurry after some new delight. . . .
>
> Equality leads by a still shorter path to the various effects I have just described.
>
> When all prerogatives of birth and fortune are abolished, when all professions are open to all and a man's own energies may bring him to the top of any one of them, an ambitious man may think it easy to launch on a great career and feel that he is called to no common destiny. But that is a delusion which experience quickly corrects. The same equality which allows each man to entertain vast hopes makes each man by himself weak. His power is limited on every side, though his longings may wander where they will.
>
> Not only are men powerless by themselves, but at every step they find immense obstacles which they had not at first noticed.

They have abolished the troublesome privileges of some of their fellows, but they come up against the competition of all. The barrier has changed shape rather than place. When men are more or less equal and are following the same path, it is very difficult for anyone of them to walk faster and get out beyond the uniform crowd surrounding and hemming them in.

This constant strive between the desires inspired by equality and the means it supplies to satisfy them harasses and wearies the mind. . . . When everything is more or less level, the slightest variation is noticed. Hence the more equal men are, the more insatiable will be their longing for equality.

Among democratic peoples men easily obtain a certain equality, but they will never get the sort of equality they long for. That is a quality which ever retreats before them without getting quite out of sight, and as it retreats it beckons them on to pursue. Every instant they think they will catch it, and each time it slips through their fingers. They see it close enough to know its charms, but they do not get near enough to enjoy it, and they will be dead before they have fully relished its delights.

That is the reason for the strange melancholy often haunting inhabitants of democracies in the midst of abundance, and of that disgust with life sometimes gripping them in calm and easy circumstances. . . .

In democratic times enjoyments are more lively than in times of aristocracy, and more especially, immeasurably greater numbers taste them. But, on the other hand, one must admit that hopes and desires are much more often disappointed, minds are more anxious and on edge, and trouble is felt more keenly.[35]

Sociologists and shrewd social observers have pointed out that the absence of unambiguous signs of status in America makes status realization difficult, status communication troublesome, and status maintenance anxiety-provoking. Thorstein Veblen called attention to the "conspicuous consumption" of parvenu upper classes, the "pecuniary canons of taste" that guided their expenditures, and the felt necessity of presenting a public appearance that accorded with their acquired station in life.[36] In a perceptive *tour de force*, Veblen devotes an entire chapter to dress, which he considers an expression of the "pecuniary culture" because "expenditure on dress has this advantage over most other methods, that our apparel is always in evidence and affords an indication of our pecuniary standing to all observers at the first glance."[37] As expressions of status anxiety, conspicuous consumption and pecuniary canons of taste are not limited to white America. Franklin Frazier has called attention to the pseudo-"society" that arises to plague Negroes who arrive in the middle class.[38] Haunted by the omnipresent stigma of race and tempted by the material prosperity available to them as prosperous persons, members of the black bourgeoisie emphasize an ultimately empty social life and a pathetically emulative high society in order to escape from the frustrations of American society. The gaudy show and ostentatious display are but dramatic props by which the middle-class Negroes seek to resolve the dilemma of their doubtful identity claims. But the problem is beyond such modes of solution: "The black bourgeoisie suffers from 'nothingness,' because when Negroes attain middle-class status, their lives generally lose both content and significance."[39]

The central conclusion to be drawn here is that in modern, formally democratic, ideally equalitarian, and highly mobile societies, new problems arise to strangle the success of those who work and achieve. More and more, they find themselves pushed toward a dramaturgic style of life. As they must demonstrate their existence, rather than live their lives; as they must seek out status rather than share their security; as they must perform in character rather than act in spontaneous ways, they experience an especially poignant estrangement and a new anxiety. The presentation of self erects invisible barriers between people, so that, distrustful of others, urged on by their own self interests, anxious to establish their own identity claims, and fearful of the consequences of naive openness, men constantly deceive one another and suffer pangs of conscience over their own social "crimes." Moreover, role performance requires an alienation from oneself, a dramatic façade which hides the "truer" self from others, and eventually (as it is stifled in its expression) from oneself as well. Only the haunting knowledge of one's own inauthenticity remains. And inauthenticity produces a fear that one will fail in role performance, reveal the baser and less creditable elements of self, and thus wreck the scene upon which the whole play of life is directed.

True, there are resolutions of these dilemmas. The grandchildren of immigrants, sensing how the gold of their forbearer's dreams has turned to dross in their own hands, seek to recover elements of the old-world culture that their parents so readily exchanged for the American promise. And persons who fill shameful or isolating statuses employ rhetorical flourishes, gestural deftness, and sign management to indicate a definitive personal style and to separate themselves from these statuses. But neither "Hansen's law of Third Generation Re-

turn"[40] nor Goffman's perceptively named stratagem of "role distance"[41] are solutions. They are mechanisms by which the fettered
drama of life is played out with less discomfort than it might
ultimately impose.

Mass
Society
and the Rhetoric
of Revolution

There is an elective affinity between the sociological reality of mass
society and the revolutionary rhetoric of contemporary students. Despite their claims of generational uniqueness, their remarkable anti-
intellectual stance, and their attack on many of the social thinkers who
have defined the problems of our time, their own ideology is a consequence of and response to the onerous conditions (real and imagined)
of mass society. The sharpness of their critique and the anxious embar-
rassment experienced by liberal-minded persons over the candor in
students' criticism serve also to heighten the vulnerability of institutions in mass society.

In a perceptive essay written two decades ago, Philip Selznick[42]
pointed to the effects of mass society on higher education. He isolated
two symptoms of massification at the university level: (1) the inability
of faculty to communicate more than expertise to their students; and
(2) the poor condition for the emergence and maintenance of intellectual elites on the campus. As a result, the university would decline
in three consecutive stages: (1) the adaptation by the faculty to the
mass character of the university; (2) the deterioration of standards of
conduct and non-technical achievement; and, finally, (3) the attenuation
of the university as a culture-bearing institution. The particular sources
of these developments, which few would disagree are occurring today,
have been described by Robert Nisbet in a denunciation of the politics
and pedagogy of certain professors supporting the New Left.[43] The
universities have succumbed to the blandishments of an "old" philistinism—*practical* considerations and *direct* service to society (in contrast to an older tradition of *intellectual* concerns and *indirect* service
to society)—and thus made themselves vulnerable to the attack of the
"new" philistinism: considerations of *relevant* education and *direct*
action in social change. When the university first agreed to teach
"practical" courses, it gave up its virgin status within the ivory tower

of intellect too eagerly. Now that it is but the handmaiden of the military-industrial complex, it cannot complain too loudly when it is raped by the angered, alienated, and vengeful offspring of its original clandestine affair. In a doleful conclusion, Nisbet asks: "In the long run, what difference does it make whether alma mater is raped from schizophrenic or merely paranoid motivations?"[44]

Socialists and liberal thinkers have written critically on this subject, applying the argument not only to universities but to the several institutions and core values that make up modern societies. Thus Selznick has pointed to the conservative role of socialist parties in defending salient aspects of American culture and principles at the same time that other elements supporting those in power called for the destruction of that culture and the abandonment of those principles.[45] Selznick predicted a new struggle within the ranks of the left over whether to chart a progressive course recognizing the roots of socialism in Western tradition and seeking to sustain the basic values of that tradition, or submerging itself in the subterranean and dark soul of anti-Western nihilism and embarking on wholesale cultural destruction:

> Ultimately we must take sides in the real struggle, which will deal harshly with our special programmatic qualifications. What, in action, will be the basic character of the movement? Will it be attuned to an essentially gradualist philosophy, with conservative precepts, with a due respect for those institutions already formed which protect and nourish our values and ideals? Or shall we build an altogether different movement, sustaining and ruled by radically different personalities, which will reach down into the emotional depths of society for the instruments of its nihilistic venture?[46]

More generally, we can see that the choice proposed by Selznick in 1944 has become in fact the dividing line between the Old Left and the New, between the liberal and the radical, between the institutionalist and the revolutionary. On the cultural level, it is the dividing line between those who wish to substitute one form of life for another and those who wish to obliterate all forms in the name of life itself.

Mass society has produced its own ethos and its own radical dialectic response to that ethos. Aspects of this ethic have been isolated: Mills describes the hollow ethics of leisure;[47] Whyte, the "social ethic";[48] Riesman, the ethic of the other-directed man;[49] and Fromm, the "marketing orientation."[50] Radical thinkers, unpersuaded of the intrinsic value of any products of the Judeo-Christian ethic or of the institutions of industrial society, seize upon these ethics as descriptions of precisely those societal elements that need to be eliminated. They are helped in this by the dialectical transformation of segmental participation—one of the principal critical concepts describing mass society—and by the vulnerability of the mass man to mobilization in behalf of an all-embracing cause.

As we have already mentioned, role performance requires the division of man into his performative parts. As Selznick defines it: "Participation is segmental when individuals interact not as whole personalities but in terms of the roles they play in the situation at hand."[51] Segmental participation is a feature of all urban, industrial, interdependent, and anonymous societies. It is the central behavioral feature and emotional astringent of mass societies. Radicals are not alone in their enunciation of the loneliness, alienation, and estrangement that comes from partial participation in social relations. But in their new ideology, the radicals seek not only to eliminate ultimately the segmentary sense of human existence, but also to reformulate tactically the image of man into a new segmentary existence. Thus it is that while the older role and status divisions of mankind are openly attacked and readily ridiculed (commitment to a status becomes enclosure in an unbefitting "bag"; attachment to a status becomes an "ego trip"), new and simplified segmentary identities are provided for those who live through the revolutionary activities. As the fight to establish "relevant" and "meaningful" ethnic studies programs becomes protracted, those who propose a scholarly consideration of issues, a gradualist approach to curricular change, and a serious search for scholarly teachers become "racists," lumped together with the reactionary elements with whom they fundamentally disagree. As the struggle between advocates of student power divides faculty colleagues from one another on a host of significant pedagogical and philosophical issues, opponents begin to operate their everyday encounters according to the "rules of irrelevance" by which nonactive identities are excluded from recognition:[52] professors become "rebels" or "establishmentarians," and all the old identity pegs which gave them numerous causes for common concern drop out in the face of the overreaching partial identity that begins to consume them. Similarly, in the sometimes guerrilla, sometimes open warfare that characterizes revolutionary student encounters with the police, the latter are transformed not into whole persons possessed by complex identities and multi-faceted existences, but rather into "pigs" deserving of nothing so much in reply to their irksome demands and orders than the guttural noise of the derogated animal itself. Marcuse has aptly commented on this dialectical rule of transformation, although without raising the issue of the dialectical usage of segmentary participation:

> Today the rupture with the linguistic universe of the Establishment is more radical; in the most militant areas of protest, it amounts to a methodical reversal of meaning. It is a familiar phenomenon that subcultural groups develop their own language, taking the harmless words of everyday communication out of their context and using them for designating objects or activities tabooed by the establishment. This is the Hippie subculture: "trip," "grass," "pot," "acid," and so on. But a far more subversive universe of discourse announces itself in the language of black militants. Here is a systematic linguistic rebellion, which smashes the ideological context in which the words are employed and defined, and places them into the opposite context —negation of the established one. Thus the blacks "take over" some of the most sublime and sublimated concepts of Western civilization, desublimate them, and redefine them. . . . The ingression of the aesthetic into the political also appears at the other pole of the rebellion against the society of affluent capitalism, among the nonconformist youth. Here, too, the reversal of meaning, driven to the point of open contradiction: giving flowers to the police, "flower power"—the redefinition and very negation of the sense of "power"; the erotic belligerency in the songs of protest; the sensuousness of long hair, of the body unsoiled by plastic cleanliness.[53]

Marcuse drives home the point of our discussion—the shrewd observation made a half-century ago by Simmel—that the aim of liberation involves the final disenchantment of all reality. In speaking of the dialectical functions served by the employment of obscenities and sexual epithets to redefine political leaders and police, he says: "And if the renaming invokes the sexual sphere, it falls in line with the great design of the desublimation of culture, which, to the radicals, is a vital aspect of liberation."[54]

Mass society is also characterized by a high degree of group involvement, coupled with a gnawing sense of incompleteness and unfulfillment. Alienated and estranged individuals seek identity with organizations, associations, groups, cliques, and gangs in order to experience a sense of holistic involvement, personal expression, and collective response. But their own and others' role orientations and personal inhibitions prevent these very goals from being realized at the same moment that they invite redoubled effort to achieve them. Hence it is that the alienated masses are manipulable into collective actions, devoid of reflective conscience, by those charismatic leaders who engulf them in mass action in the name of personal liberation. The person experiencing a segmental self might realize the advantages of his multiplied identities and separated performances for the realization of a private sense of freedom and solitude, but in the rhetoric of the current revolution, this personal pluralism goes unmentioned and unhallowed. In its stead we find not the transcendent person protected by his roles from the importunities of fate or fortune, but rather the submerged alienate, plunged into the crowd, moved by the monotonous thrill of demagogy, seeking in mass action a liberation through the abolition of his massness.

Notes

[1]Max Weber, *The Protestant Ethic and the Spirit of Capitalism* (New York: Charles Scribner, 1930), pp. 181-82.

[2]See Ortega y Gasset, *The Revolt of the Masses* (London: Unwin Books, 1961), pp. 96-144.

[3]See Hannah Arendt, *The Human Condition* (Garden City: Doubleday Anchor, 1959), p. 48.

[4]See Erich Fromm, *Man for Himself* (New York: Holt, Rinehart, and Winston, 1947), pp. 67-82. See also two works by Robert A. Nisbet, *Community and Power* (New York: Oxford Galaxy, 1962), esp. pp. 3-74, and *The Sociological Tradition* (New York: Basic Books, 1966), pp. 47-106.

[5]See Herbert Blumer, "Collective Behavior," in *New Outline in the Principles of Sociology*, ed. Alfred McClung Lee (New York: Barnes and Noble, 1946), pp. 185-89.

[6]See Georg Simmel, "The Metropolis and Mental Life," in *The Sociology of Georg Simmel*, ed. and trans. Kurt H. Wolff (Glencoe: The Free Press, 1950), pp. 409-24.

[7]Robert E. Park, "Community Organization and Juvenile Delinquency," in *The City*, eds. Robert E. Park, et al. (Chicago: University of Chicago Press, 1967), p. 107.

[8]*Ibid.*, p. 109.

[9]*Ibid.*, p. 117.

[10]*Loc. cit.*

[11]Daniel Bell, "America as a Mass Society," in *The End of Ideology* (New York: Collier Books, 1961), pp. 21-22.

[12]*Ibid.*, pp. 22-25.

[13]William Kornhauser, *The Politics of Mass Society* (Glencoe: The Free Press, 1959), pp. 21-101.

[14]See Edward Shils, "The Theory of Mass Society," in *America as a Mass Society*, ed. Philip Olson (New York: The Free Press of Glencoe, 1963), pp. 30-50.

[15]Sigmund Freud, "Mourning and Melancholy," *Collected Papers*, trans. Joan Riviere (New York: Basic Books, 1959), IV, 153.

[16]Portions of the following appear in slightly different form in our essay, "Accounts, Deviance, and Social Order," in *Deviance and Respectability*, ed. Jack D. Douglas (New York: Basic Books, 1970).

[17]See Marvin B. Scott and Stanford M. Lyman, "Accounts," *American Sociological Review*, XXXIII (February, 1968), 46-62.

[18]Milton M. Gordon, *Assimilation in American Life* (New York: Oxford University Press, 1964), p. 158.

[19]For a discussion of the idea of communalism, see J. A. Laponce, *The Protection of Minorities*, University of California Publications in Political Science (Berkeley: University of California Press, 1960), IX, 84.

[20]See J. S. Furnivall, *Colonial Policy and Practice* (New York: New York University Press, 1956), pp. 303-12; and Lord Lugard, *The Dual Mandate in British Tropical Africa* (Hamden, Conn.: Archon Books, 1965), pp. 193-229.

[21]For a discussion and illustration of this point, see Pierre van den Berghe, *South Africa* (Berkeley: University of California Press, 1967), p. 267.

[22]See Everett C. Hughes and Helen M. Hughes, *Where Peoples Meet* (Glencoe: Free Press, 1952).

[23]For an illustration of the point, see Leonard Covello, *The Social Background of the Italo-American School Child* (Leiden: E. J. Brill, 1967), pp. 277-79.

[24]For a classic statement, see Ferdinand Tonnies, *Community and Society*, trans. and ed. Charles P. Loomis (East Lansing: The Michigan State University Press, 1957), pp. 251ff.

[25]For a full statement of these styles, see Martin Joos, *The Five Clocks* (New York: Harbinger Books, 1961).

[26]Talcott Parsons, *The Social System* (Glencoe: The Free Press, 1951), p. 189.

[27]This theme has been brilliantly explored in the plays and stories of Tennessee Williams. For a particularly bizarre example, see his "Desire and the Black Masseur," in *One Arm and Other Stories* (New York: New Directions, 1954), pp. 83-96.

[28]See Willard Gaylin, "Epilogue: The Meaning of Despair," in *The Meaning of Despair: Psychoanalytic Contributions to the Understanding of Depression*, ed. Willard Gaylin (New York: Science House, 1968), p. 388.

[29]Erving Goffman, *The Presentation of Self in Everyday Life* (Garden City: Doubleday Anchor, 1959).

[30]See Stanford M. Lyman and Marvin B. Scott, "Coolness in Everyday Life," in *Sociology and Everyday Life*, ed. Marcello Truzzi (Englewood Cliffs, N. J.: Prentice-Hall, 1968), pp. 92-101.

[31]See Marvin B. Scott and Stanford M. Lyman, "Paranoia, Homosexuality, and Game Theory," *Journal of Health and Social Behavior*, IX (September, 1968), 179-87. For the concept "bad faith," see Jean-Paul Sartre, *Being and Nothingness*, trans. Hazel E. Barnes (New York: Philosophical Library, 1956), pp. 47-72.

[32]The following quotes are taken from Robert E. Park, "Human Nature and Collective Behavior," in *Society, The Collected Papers of Robert E. Park*, ed. Everett C. Hughes, et al. (Glencoe: The Free Press, 1955), III, 13-21.

[33]For a full discussion, see "Stage Fright and the Problem of Identity," in Stanford M. Lyman and Marvin B. Scott, *A Sociology of the Absurd* (New York: Appleton-Century-Crofts, 1970).

[34]See Seymour Martin Lipset and Reinhard Bendix, *Social Mobility in Industrial Society* (Berkeley: University of California Press, 1959); and Seymour Martin Lipset, *The First New Nation* (New York: Basic Books, 1963).

[35]Alexis de Tocqueville, *Democracy in America*, eds. J. P. Mayer and Max Lerner (New York: Harper and Row, 1966), pp. 509-11.

[36]Thorstein Veblen, *The Theory of the Leisure Class* (New York: Mentor, 1953).

[37]*Ibid.*, p. 119.

[38]E. Franklin Frazier, *Black Bourgeoisie* (Glencoe: The Free Press, 1957).

[39]*Ibid.*, p. 238.

[40]See Marcus Lee Hansen, "The Problem of the Third Generation Immigrant," Augustana Historical Society, 1938, reprinted in *Commentary*, XIV (November, 1952), 492-500. See also Eugene Bender and George Kagiwada, "Hansen's Law of 'Third-Generation Return' and the Study of American Religio-Ethnic Groups," *Phylon Quarterly* (Fourth Quarter, 1968), pp. 360-70.

[41]Erving Goffman, "Role Distance," in *Encounters* (Indianapolis: Bobbs-Merrill, 1961), pp. 85-152.

[42]Philip Selznick, "Institutional Vulnerability in Mass Society," in *America as a Mass Society*, ed. Philip Olson (New York: The Free Press of Glencoe, 1963), pp. 13-29.

[43]Robert A. Nisbet, "The New Philistinism," *Trans-Action*, VI (May, 1969), 54-56. See also his essays on the subject in *Tradition and Revolt* (New York: Random House, 1968).

[44]*Ibid.*, p. 55.

[45]Philip Selznick, "Revolution Sacred and Profane," in *The Anarchists*, ed. Irving L. Horowitz (New York: Dell, 1964), pp. 562-72.

[46]*Ibid.*, pp. 566-67.

[47]C. Wright Mills, *White Collar* (New York: Oxford Galaxy, 1956), pp. 235-38.

[48]William H. Whyte, *The Organization Man* (Garden City: Doubleday Anchor, 1956).

[49]David Riesman, Nathan Glazer and Reuel Denny, *The Lonely Crowd* (Garden City: Doubleday Anchor, 1950).

[50]Erich Fromm, *Man for Himself* (New York: Holt, Rinehart, and Winston, 1947), pp. 67-82.

[51]Selznick, "Institutional Vulnerability in Mass Society," *op. cit.*, p. 20.

[52]Goffman, "Fun in Games," in *Encounters* (Indianapolis: Bobbs-Merrill, 1961).

[53]Herbert Marcuse, *An Essay on Liberation* (Boston: Beacon Press, 1969), pp. 34-36.

[54]*Ibid.*, p. 35n.

Chapter III
the Nature
of the Ideology

Ideologies are conceptual schemes that clarify the world at the same time they hope to change it. Ideologies provide for their adherents a persistent description of the world and a plethora of evidence to validate that description. Historical events, current affairs, and future happenings are perceptually organized and this, in turn, reacts to help achieve persistent belief in the ideology itself.

All ideologies have their ideologues, intellectual lightning rods who attract to themselves disciples and followers, elucidators and practitioners—men who devote themselves to clarifying the original point and living out the promise of the ideological prophecy. The current student movement is no exception. Just as there is a general ideology as well as specific concrete ideologies, so also are there general ideologues who may be matched with their lesser counterparts, intellectuals engaged in concrete critiques of society. Thus, in the following, we shall distinguish between those intellectuals who present a more or less total critique of society and those "specialists" who concentrate on specific concrete social arrangements. The former provide the general frame of reference within which the more specific perspectives may be established. The latter provide an amplification and deepening of the general position.

A century ago, Marx suggested that the specter of communism was haunting Europe. In our time, that specter has been diffuse, all but banished from its old haunts, but in its place is a vague, but powerful dread—not so much of things to come, but rather of things as they are and are likely to continue to be. The dread is of alienation.

Alienation is the root metaphor of our time. And community is the utopian ideal.[1] Man everywhere seems to sense that he could be freer than he is; at the same time, he lacks the power to create this newly desired freedom. Man everywhere seems to sense that the world is absurd, meaningless, devoid of sensibility; at the same time, he lacks the cognitive acumen by which to comprehend it. Man everywhere feels detached from meaningful associations; at the same time, he feels socially ignorant of how to establish a secure *Gemeinschaft*. Man everywhere senses the irrelevance of norms governing conduct; at the same time, he lacks the courage to face an unpredictable world. Man everywhere seems to feel not only attenuated from society but also estranged from himself; at the same time, he does not know how to restore his emotional equilibrium nor to achieve personal harmony. The general ideologists of the current revolt have developed the theme of social, political, and personal estrangement as the source, and a new socially and personally fulfilling community as the objective of the new movement.

Politics and psychology provide the parameters of the new intellectual perspective. Two of the principal ideologues of this perspective are C. Wright Mills and Erich Fromm. According to Mills,[2] there is in America a relatively invulnerable power elite composed of industrial directors, military leaders, and political officials who make the "important" (i.e., the life-and-death) decisions for the nation. This oligarchy rules over a sham-democracy whose citizens are either tricked into believing they still share decision-making powers by participating in seemingly important "veto groups," or they are titillated and amused by a dream factory (i.e., Hollywood and the celebrities), which spends their energies on apolitical activities and obfuscates their view of the actual state of power and dependency in which they live. The new result is a "higher immorality" on the part of the elite on the one hand, and a deepening chasm between the exercise of power and the will of the people on the other. As Mills concludes: "The men of the higher circles are not representative men; their position is not one of moral virtue; their fabulous success is not firmly connected with meritorious ability. . . . Commanders of power unequaled in human history, they have succeeded within the American system of organized irresponsibility."[3]

If, for Mills, the American polity has produced an estrangement between people and power, civilized society has produced for Fromm an estrangement between man and himself. The process of maturation, Fromm observes, has two aspects: on the one hand, the child increases his physical, emotional, and mental strength; on the other hand, he experiences greater and greater individuation and aloneness—a gnawing sense of impotence and detachment from the community. This latter characteristic is the most problematical, leading, in individual and collective extreme cases, to abject submission to authority and a voluntary renunciation of freedom.[4] However, the terror of aloneness is enhanced by doctrines and structural arrangements—by Luther's and Calvin's doctrine of man's powerlessness and evil nature, by the anguish of apparently insoluble mass unemployment, and by the dread of seemingly inevitable and unending wars.[5] Over the years, Fromm developed his argument even further so that with the publication of his essay "Psychoanalysis and Zen Buddhism"[6] in 1960, he stressed that man is deprived of contact with and an awareness of reality by the basic elements of civilization itself, language, logic, and social inhibition. The result is a crippling of the human perspective and a transmutation of the "content of consciousness [into that which] is mostly fictional and delusional."[7] The villain that has maimed man's consciousness and deprived him of meaningful communion is society itself: "[Most] of what is in our consciousness is 'false consciousness' and . . . it is essentially society that fills us with these fictitious and unreal notions."[8] As John Schaar has summed up Fromm's position:

> With these formulations, Fromm in effect converts all known social orders into so many prisons, places in which each individual is locked in his own cell, isolated from his fellows by the delusions of consciousness, and brought into a vicious and alienated contact with the "community" only during the scheduled periods of collective recreation and work. . . . Fromm here sees society only as a force which cripples, corrupts, confines. Any collective smaller than the universal brotherhood of love is too small for universal man.[9]

The proper solution, it appears from Fromm's analysis, is a restoration of spontaneity and love through the abolition of society's mediating—and thus stultifying—institutions. For Fromm and for some of his followers, this would be done not by a direct act of destruction, but rather by one of affirmation. But for others caught up in the belief that society is incarceration, only a demolition of the prison itself would insure permanent liberty.

What Mills and Fromm provide is a radical critique of society organized around the paired concepts[10] of the people and the polity and man and society, respectively. In both the relationships of the populace to politics and of the individual to his fellow men, they argue, there has been an unwarranted separation. And in both instances the institutions of society have proved to be either knavish or foolish, either too powerful or not influential enough. Thus the mediating institutions of American mass society—clubs, associations, unions, and cliques—are too constraining on man's spirit which longs for liberation; but at the same time they are too impotent to prevent the real power holders (i.e., the Establishment) from having their way in the face of man's contrary wishes. From the synthesis (and the distortions as well) of this double-edged critique have been forged the special ideologies which, in loose confraternity, make up the fundamental ideas of the students in revolt.

The current student revolt has produced its own intellectual representatives and partisans. Unlike Mills and Fromm, these men are, for the most part, occasional participants in, as well as programmers of, the revolt. Moreover, while these men borrow from and build on the ideas of Mills and Fromm, they tend to specialize their efforts of authorship and action in one arena of society, and to push toward "liberation" in the one sphere while giving moral support and occasional physical aid and financial support to the others. In general, there is one theme that overrides their specific approaches—fight the "system"; put down the Establishment.

The current students and their allies are not the only ones to have attacked the established institutions and traditional verities. Indeed, while general critiques have been abundant, at least one outspoken critic—William H. Whyte, Jr.—set out a program whereby young people entering into middle-management posts in the enlarging corporate structure of American occupations could cheat on personality tests.[11] Yet Whyte's plans for subversion of corporate personnel surveillance did not arouse widespread enthusiasm, nor did it raise a significant outcry. Moreover, in the past century a certain number of white intellectuals and "bohemians" have dropped out of society, becoming hoboes, forming colonies in the hinterlands, establishing intellectual communities in the cities, or migrating to expatriate refuges in Europe. Similarly, since their first years in the New World, Negroes have shifted efforts among a search for integration and liberty within American society, the establishment of Black utopias, colonization in unsettled areas, expatriate exile, and a "Zionist" interest in resettlement in Africa. Yet none of these movements appears to have aroused the public in quite so hostile a manner, nor to have brought down upon themselves such a legion of opposed force, as has the current student revolt. What separates all these critiques and movements from the current revolt in their respective orientations toward the social order? To begin with, we may roughly distinguish between rebels and revolutionaries. Rebels accept the legitimacy of the social order but attack particular features; revolutionaries oppose the fundamental order itself. Now, in Whyte's proposal to cheat on personality tests, we have a minor rebellion, but no revolution. In the hippie movement, we have the individual withdrawal of human services, but no direct and sustained attack on the social order. In the utopian colonies, we have perhaps a potential revolution by imitation, but their cloistered location tends to remove them from the public eye. Expatriate and migratory movements combine rejection of the system with withdrawal from active involvement with it. In short, none of these other "attacks" on the system threatened its wholesale existence. But, endowed with an ideology that opposes institutional arrangements as such, and willing to take direct action, the students in revolt are just the kind of threat to arouse major counteractive forces.

Among the in-group ideologists, there is no single person who stands out. Instead, and consistent with the anti-formalism inherent in its outlook, there are "area specialists" who set forth the critique and claims of the sector of the population they represent. With certain important exceptions, there are few fully developed articulations of the current ideology. The Port Huron Statement[12] comes closest to a general statement of guidelines for the current revolt, but it still does not embrace the breadth of the Movement. For the rest we have specific statements, speeches, pamphlets, open letters, and short essays. We can nevertheless attempt a tentative list of the current radical ideologues and their links to specific areas of concern.

Among the more general ideologists are certain intellectuals who, while they may take only an occasional part in direct action, provide ideational justification and moral encouragement to the Movement. Included here are Herbert Marcuse, Paul Goodman, and Staughton Lynd.[13] A second sector of ideological support arises from those already dead movement leaders, all Black or foreign, but by no means in agreement with one another, who are both martyrs and guides to its contemporary social direction: Frantz Fanon, Malcolm X, Martin Luther King, Jr., and Che Guevara.[14] Finally, there are those who, at this writing, are still active in leading and writing for the student revolt. Included here are Tom Hayden, Jerry Rubin, Abbie Hoffman, Mark Rudd, and Mario Savio (Students for a Democratic Society, student liberation); Stokely Carmichael, Charles V. Hamilton, and Nathan Hare (black liberation and power); and Daniel Cohn-Bendit (student revolt in Europe; post-communist Marxism).[15] Others may yet arise, but it would be inconsistent with the general formlessness of the new ideal of freedom for a single ideologue to take intellectual command of the whole movement.

the Content
of Current
Ideology

To be effective, an ideology must have a new terminology, a language or a dialect that is not only fashionable but that fashions new labels and new meanings for current affairs and existing institutions. By its novel language, ideology unites hitherto diverse groups and separated individuals, providing a common bond of identity and interest and a common focus for action. In Marxian terms, an effective ideology is one that can transform an aggregate into a class, and animate that class into group-serving action—that is, transform an *an sich* into a *für sich*. Some of the new terms are student power, black power, power to the people, self-determination, liberation; hang-ups, uptight, and do-your-own-thing; relevance, local control, and love not war. These terms are "signature" words to the Movement whose fundamental dimensions can be abstracted through careful examination of them and their referents.

Three themes are prominent in the current ideology although different segments of the movement may emphasize one more than any other: *autonomy, humane compassion, and social and intellectual relevance*. We shall examine each of these themes in terms of its specific belief system, its existential (i.e., the way things are) and normative (i.e., the way things should be) beliefs,[16] and its particular formulation to the various subgroups that make up the Movement.

Autonomy

Throughout the current movement we hear demands for personal freedom, group independence, and general liberation from legal restraints, customary controls, and social inhibitions. The belief system here is the obverse side of the theme of powerlessness. Men are impotent to influence public policy or personal life under current arrangements. As a result, political life is perceived as oppressive. Citizens are effectively enjoined from their civic opportunities at the same time that they are reminded of their patriotic duties.

Autonomy promises a fundamental shift in the political arrangements among men. In its most general sense autonomy will convert fatalistic helplessness into humanistic potency. Men will recover their lost power to challenge fate, control destiny, and manage affairs. Instead of one or several oligarchical power elites controlling human action, power itself will become diffused and distributed over mankind in general so that each individual senses his own mastery over his own life. Whereas the political arrangements of advanced societies relegate ordinary man to resignation or desperation, when autonomy has been established neither dreaded helplessness nor ill-fated acts of liberation will be necessary. Man will be able to do, think, and act as he pleases, unfettered by rules, roles, or regulations.

Existential Beliefs. As Parsons has defined them, the existential ideas of any system of beliefs are descriptions of the external world or its parts, of entities now existent, existent at some time in the past, or likely to become existent.[17] The existential ideas that prompt the theme of autonomy are the claims that the United States is controlled by an oligarchical power elite, composed of the corporate leadership of the military-industrial complex and its subordinated but supportive political officials. In addition to this elite's relative invulnerability to criticism, its ownership or control of the means of media production, its repressive intolerance of heretical dissent, and its enormous capacity for destruction make it the source of individual man's sense of impotence. Side by side with the economic-military-political power elite are other institutional elites that, each in its own particular arena of control, suborn freedom and support the repressive *status quo.* Thus business and labor, both beneficiaries of the material wealth of advanced industrial development, have grown more amicable and less antagonistic toward one another, while each secures advantages arising from the neglect of the poor and oppressed and the support of terrifying foreign wars. Churches and religious establishments, freed from direct interference from the state, have repaid their debt by raising no effective challenge to the state and by silencing or suborning their own dissident clergy. Universities and colleges, once seats of truth and places of wisdom, are now "multi-versities" that have compromised the search for truth and the enunciation of wisdom in the name of service to community or national elites. Power is everywhere rooted in possession, privilege, or circumstance, and those who fall outside these three domains are left in a felt state of despair, despondency and desperation.

The Port Huron Statement of the Students for a Democratic Society is an excellent presentation of these ideas. It contains an interpretation of history, an analysis of values, a statement about the nature of man, and a description of an appropriate polity. It also analyzes the role of students in the present and future society. Its existential ideas are contained in the discussions of history, values, polity, and students—discussions that shade off frequently into normative statements as well. Its opening words[18] present a priority of time and circumstance that embraces the current mood: "We are the people of this generation, bred in at least modest comfort, housed now in universities, looking uncomfortably to the world we inherit."

Relevant history, for the writers of the statement, begins with their outlook on the world when they were children and changes dramatically and fundamentally as they become mature and socially conscious. "When we were kids," the Statement begins with a naiveté and touchingness that bespeaks the youthful affection that animates this section, "the United States was the wealthiest and strongest country in the world; the only one with the atom bomb, the least scarred by modern war, an initiator of the United Nations that we thought would distribute Western influence throughout the world." Faith in the childlike promise of universal Occidental beneficence at first gave rise to optimism: "Freedom and equality for each individual, government of, by, and for the people—these American values we found good, principles by which we could live as men." And this optimism has another effect: "Many of us began maturing in complacency."

However, with the onset of maturity two problems became very real for the young students who were later to put their signatures to the Port Huron Statement. First was the recognition of human degradation symbolized by, but by no means confined to, the response of the South to the new drive for civil rights for Negroes; second was the anguished sense of fear, dread, and fatalism inspired by the seemingly insoluble Cold War and the unparalleled doom ordained by thermonuclear war. These twin problems forced recognition of several "paradoxes" in the American system: "The declaration 'all men are created equal . . .' rang hollow before the facts of Negro life in the South and the big cities of the North. The proclaimed peaceful intentions of the United States contradicted its economic and military investment in the Cold War status quo." These paradoxes, once realized, opened up an entire set of related "paradoxes," existential contradictions in America and the world:

> With nuclear energy whole cities can easily be powered, yet the dominant nation-states seem more likely to unleash destruction greater than that incurred in all wars of human history. Although our own technology is destroying old and creating new forms of social organization, men still tolerate meaningless words and idleness. While two-thirds of mankind suffers undernourishment, our own upper classes revel amidst superfluous abundance. Although world population is expected to double in forty years, the nations still tolerate anarchy as a major principle of international conduct and uncontrolled exploitation governs the sapping of the earth's physical resources. Although mankind desperately needs revolutionary leadership, America rests in national stalemate, its goals ambiguous and tradition bound instead of informed and clear, its democratic system apathetic and manipulated rather than "of, by, and for the people."

Finally, the Port Huron Statement defines the present in such a way as to give it an absolute primacy over past or future: "Our work is guided by the sense that we may be the last generation in the experiment with living." Yet despite their own sense of urgency and immediacy, the young people who met at Port Huron believed that the bulk of Americans did not share their general perspective or their apprehensions for the future:

> But we are a minority. . . . In this is perhaps the outstanding paradox: we ourselves are imbued with urgency, yet the message of our society is that there is no viable alternative to the present. Beneath the reassuring tones of the politicians, beneath the common opinion that America will "muddle through," beneath the stagnation of those who have closed their minds to the future, is the pervading feeling that there simply are no alternatives, that our times have witnessed the exhaustion not only of Utopias, but of any new departures as well.

The actual thrust of the American mind, according to the Statement, is one of fearful paralysis with respect to innovative thought and creative reconstruction:

> Feeling the press of complexity upon the emptiness of life, people are fearful of the thought that at any moment things might

be thrust out of control. They fear change itself, since change might smash whatever invisible framework seems to hold back chaos for them now. For most Americans all crusades are suspect, threatening. The fact that each individual sees apathy in his fellows perpetuates the common reluctance to organize for change. The dominant institutions are complex enough to blunt the minds of their potential critics, and entrenched enough to swiftly dissipate or entirely repel the energies of protest and re- form, thus limiting human expectancies. Then too we are dra- matically improving society and by our own improvements we seem to have weakened the case for further change.

Among their nonempirical existential ideas, the Students for a Democratic Society include an analysis of values and the American polity. The enunciation of values has been debased by the corruption of language and institutions. In lieu of explicit and clear values Ameri- can policy is pursued in the name of patriotic slogans and war cries. And in this devaluation of morality, the political establishment is not alone:

> But neither has our experience in the universities brought us moral enlightenment. Our professors and administrators sacrifice controversy to public relations; their curriculums change more slowly than the living events of the world; their skills and silence are purchased by investors in the arms race; passion is called unscholastic. . . . Unlike youth in other countries we are used to moral leadership being exercised and moral dimensions being clarified by our elders. But today, for us, not even the liberal and socialist preachments of the past seem adequate to the forms of the present.

The empirical ideas about American politics, however, set the cap- stone on the Port Huron convention's analysis of the lack of autonomy in America. Instead of being "the democratic model of which its glorifiers speak," the American political system actually "frustrates democracy by confusing the individual citizen, paralyzing policy dis- cussion, and consolidating the irresponsible power of military and business interests." The American party system blunts real conflicts by harboring greater differences within the parties than exist between them. Moreover, local party rule deflects discussion away from serious issues at the same time that whole constituencies—especially Negroes —are denied representation and the franchise. Furthermore, the huge lobbying interests of business give them a disproportionate power to the disadvantage of less affluent groups. The net result of all of this is "a politics without publics," isolating the individual from power, community, and even the aspiration to change the system. "With the great mass of people structurally remote and psychologically hesitant with respect to democratic institutions, those institutions themselves attenuate and become, in the fashion of the vicious circle, progressively less accessible to those few who aspire to serious participation in social affairs."

The situation of the American college student is a crucial instance of the general malaise of America. Although students have recently taken part in freedom rides, sit-ins, strikes, and demonstrations, this only signifies a crack in the crust of apathy and alienation that is an inherent part of American college life. The institutions of higher learning in America are not only paid handmaidens of the military-industrial complex, but they also adopt a paternalistic attitude toward education denigrating it in both content and spirit. Student extra-curricular activity is an exercise in political pretense. In the language of Berkeley's SLATE, a precursor of the FSM, student politics was a "sand-box" affair devoid of issues and stultified by a substitution of popularity contests for political debate. Students lose their identities as individuals and are transformed into spiritless numbers ground forth, classified, and programmed by giant computers. University curricula, judged according to the practices of administrators and teachers, exist solely for the production of new human robots to be hired, exploited, and ultimately retired by the mammoth industrial and military behemoth.

Normative Beliefs. "An idea is normative," according to Parsons, "insofar as the maintenance or attainment of the state of affairs it describes may be regarded as an end of the actor."[19] The normative ideas of any movement constitute the "utopias" toward which its ideology is directed. With respect to autonomy, the Movement promises a liberation of man from victimization and control by oligarchical, bureaucratic and inhumane institutions. More particularly it hopes to expand the horizons of human experience by unshackling man from inhibitions imposed by custom or institutions. The general form of man's alienation is a product of these inhibitions producing in him a sense of loneliness, estrangement, and isolation. However, since men "have an unrealized potential for self-cultivation, self-direction, self-understanding, and creativity" their lives can be so transformed that this potential is realized:

> We would replace power rooted in possession, privilege, or circumstance by power and uniqueness rooted in love, reflectiveness, reason, and creativity. As a *social system* we seek the

establishment of a democracy of individual participation, governed by two central aims: that the individual share in those
social decisions determining the quality and direction of his life;
that society be organized to encourage independence in men
and provide the media for their common participation.

Participatory democracy in the political, economic, educational spheres
—indeed in all spheres of life—will create an acceptable pattern of
social relations, restore community by re-establishing meaning in individual life, and provide solutions not only for pressing social, political,
and economic problems, but also for personal difficulties.

Subgroup Variations. "The leitmotifs that dominate the Movement,"
write Jacobs and Landau, "extend far beyond politics. The Movement
is much more than anti-Vietnam marches, civil rights demonstrations,
and student sit-ins. To be in the Movement is to search for a psychic
community, in which one's own identity can be defined, social and
personal relationships based on love can be established and can grow,
unfettered by the cramping pressures of the careers and life styles so
characteristic of America today."[20] Autonomy in the movement is
achieved or aimed at in various ways. Here we shall distinguish three:
student power, psychic communion and the expansion of consciousness,
and cultural nationalism.

Student power seeks to establish rights of decision-making in academic areas hitherto held to be within the sole domain of faculties,
administrators, boards of trustees, and state or local governments.[21]
Particularly important here are control over and change in the curricular
contents and the recruitment, promotion, and retention of faculty. At
the same time that the Movement aims at establishing participatory
democracy in the university, it moves in the immediate direction of
establishing para-university curricula, established, taught, and attended
by students (and a few fellow-traveling instructors). These are the
so-called "free universities" in which new subjects, new modes of teaching and learning and intensive discussion and dialogue take place.
Beyond the curriculum and its instructors is the interest in converting
the university from an inactive role (the ivory tower) or from a subordinated supporter of current social, economic, and political policies
(the multiversity) into an active agency of social change. Student
elections are urged to focus on "serious" issues—the elimination of
ROTC; the abolition of university cooperation with draft boards,
industries producing war materials, and military recruiting services; and
the establishment of unlimited freedom of speech and political activity.

Finally, elections themselves are suspect, and hence the Movement advocates the maintenance of demonstrations and other activities of direct political expression, and of a collective bargaining arrangement between students and administration.

Much of the new thrust of the Movement is toward a liberation from personal anxiety and social estrangement through various modes of communion and consciousness expansion. Foremost among the former are the several kinds of voluntary and non-professional group therapy approaches that are not only supported by elements of the Movement but also by non-Movement segments of the business and teaching worlds.[22] Whether conducted as Synanon games, T-groups, buzz sessions, sensitivity training, or encounter groups, the common theme of these therapies is a breakdown of the socially created edifices of role orientation and the liberation of the "true" self through direct uninhibited expression. In addition these therapy groups are counter-elitist in the sense that their very operation denies the significance or efficacy of special or professional knowledge and also in the fact that, in most cases, when professionals are employed as "leaders," they tend to function in a passive or permissive manner. The self that emerges out of the lengthy, painful, emotion-laden, sometimes brutal sessions that are a commonplace of this strand of the Movement is supposedly liberated from the shibboleths of social roles, freed from the constraints of taboos and customs, and endowed with the capacity for both psychological self-sufficiency and effective community.

Consciousness expansion is further effected by the use of drugs. Although the currently much vaunted pleasures and perceptions obtainable from the injection or ingestion of pot, hash, speed or smack were once only recognized by European bohemians, American eccentrics, Chinese laborers, and Negro musicians, much of the Movement —but not all of it—is dedicated to personal and group indulgence in drug use and to legitimating and legalizing the possession and distribution of drugs. A special set of existential and normative beliefs accompanies this segment of the Movement. Drug use is alleged to be not only euphoric but harmless. Its dangers are said to be less than those derived from tobacco or alcohol. Ideologues count generally recognized famous men among the users of opiates in the past and imply that their success was at least in part a function of their ingestion of drugs. Finally, the newly discovered hallucinogens, especially Lysergic Acid, are praised for their peculiar quality of separating consciousness from time and space and for permitting the user to experience a special kind of adventure—a trip or excursion into the unknown realms of consciousness and character—while remaining externally bound to the physical and social space which embrace his conventional environment. Autonomy here is aided by drugs and experienced as an interior set of sensations: an escape from the fatalistic here-and-now by an inner voyage to freedom and spontaneity.

Another and far more active and distinct expression of autonomy occurs in the various modes of cultural nationalism that have sprung up primarily among America's national and racial minorities. The most prominent but by no means the only movement of this kind is the Black Power movement. This movement itself is purposefully vague, referring not so much to any single program or plan but rather to a variety of ideas and moods, perceptions and policies, that have as their goal the establishment of freedom and self-determination for the black population of America. Within the all-embracing *élan* of Black Power are political separatism, community self-determination, black voting blocs, and Negro constituencies; economic autarchy, black industry, Negro cooperatives, and community controlled wars on poverty; black universities, Afro-American curricula, Negro history, and ethnic study programs; black identity, Afro-American sociology, Swahili and other African languages, and the conversion of the descendants of slaves from Negroes to blacks.

While Black Power has generated the most discussion and notoriety, demands for power, community, and positive ethnic identity have arisen among the youth of Indian, Mexican-American, Chinese-American, Japanese-American, and Puerto Rican groups. Indians speak of "Red Power" and plan on securing a greater voice in the policies of the Bureau of Indian Affairs; Mexican-American youth sport brown berets, speak of themselves as *Chicanos* and people of *La Raza*, demand recognition of their peculiar history and culture, and denounce historians and sociologists for their reiteration of the theme of evolution and emergence rather than action and contribution in studies of Mexicans in the United States; Oriental-Americans pin "Yellow Peril" buttons to their jackets, demand college programs in Asian studies, and offer radical, reformist, and eleemosynary aid to their less fortunate brethren in the ghettos of Chinatown and *Nihonmachi*; Puerto Ricans think about national self-determination for their island homeland and anguish over whether to join with or keep separate from their more militant and sometimes better organized black compatriots. Under the umbrella of the Third World Liberation Front all these now nationally self-conscious minorities combine together to protest the intellectual obliteration, psychic deterioration, social neglect, and individual demoralization of America's non-white peoples. Power and pride can restore the life of these peoples. Power will secure rights, opportunities, and protection; pride will secure group consciousness, individual confidence, and collective self-service.

The autonomy sought here stands in sharp contrast to the ideal of integration officially celebrated by but only occasionally realized in the larger society. Louis Wirth once observed that minority groups would eventually assimilate if only they were given the opportunity to experience autonomy within a recognized pluralistic society.[23] If this is correct, then the current assertion of cultural, social, political, and economic autonomy is the most significant development of this pluralism in the modern era. But it is by no means clear that the various forms of ethnic nationalism current in America are aiming at a phase of national consciousness prerequisite to full-scale assimilation into the larger order. Rather, the principal argument of the new nationalism includes a fundamental critique of American society holding it to be inherently racist. Furthermore, assimilation itself is judged to be a cloak for benevolent and liberal white racism, seeking to absorb all peoples into the culture and class of the Anglo-Saxon Protestant and obliterate the cherished values and peculiar institutions of the several ethnic groups that actually comprise American society.

At universities and colleges the search for ethnic liberation takes a special direction—the demand for separate, autonomous, ethnic colleges devoted to study of, by, and for national minorities. Originally a demand for academic restoration and recognition of those cultures and histories that have been systematically obliterated from the general cultural consciousness by neglect and intellectual racism, a radical version of ethnic studies demands that the curriculum not merely present the historic and cultural past but also and more significantly play a direct role in shaping the present and formulating the future of the particular race in question. Thus the curriculum is to be coordinated with the concerns of the community, and, conversely, the community, now recognized as possessed of reason and capacity for self-determination, is to choose its academic leaders and to set the tone and terms of intellectual inquiry.

Student power, psychic communion and the expansion of consciousness, and cultural nationalism are but particular aims of the general assertion of life over form. Ultimately the aim remains to act in accordance with the single most important motto of the movement—"do your own thing." Thus, Abbie Hoffman, one of the most forceful exponents of the Movement has written:

Our message is always: Do what you want. Take chances. Protest is anything you can get away with. Don't get paranoid.
Don't be uptight. We are a gang of theatrical cheerleaders, yell-
ing Go! Go! Go! We serve as symbols of liberation.[24]

Humane Compassion

A second and much older ideal animating current unrest is humane
compassion. Certainly there is nothing new in principle here. Rather
there is on the one hand a critique of social thought for relegating
humane compassion to the dustheap of intellectual endeavor, for
redefining social amelioration as non-productive *Weltschmerz*, and
for asserting neutral "objectivity" as the single most important criterion
of social science; on the other hand there is a social backlash to the
announcement of America as an affluent society—the rediscovery of
poverty and pariahs, coexistent with and suffering from the exploitative
operations of that affluence.

"It is ironic," writes Carey McWilliams, "that at a time when the
possibility of actually creating a utopia, any kind of utopia, did not
exist—for lack of know-how and wherewithal—the projection of utopias
was a favorite pastime of historians, scientists, philosophers, and states-
man. . . . Today we have, as never before, the resources, the wealth,
the science, the technology, the organizational skills which could be
used to fashion utopias without end. . . . Yet despite the prodigious
resources now available, utopias have gone out of fashion; indeed anti-
utopias are 'in,' and utopias are 'out.' "[25] Humane compassion for the
poor and misbegotten at one time served to inspire social science in
America. Lester Ward, perhaps the single most important American
theorist of social betterment through social science, once commanded
considerable attention in American intellectual, liberal, and revolutionary circles; today his concept of "social telesis," despite its linguistic
suitability to a heavily jargonized sociology, has fallen into total dis-
use.[26] In place of meliorism in social science and utopia in social politics
there have arisen the twin precepts of objectivity and compromise.

Objectivity calls upon the scientist, but even more upon the student-
scientist, to suspend his interest in society, inhibit his evaluative capacities, eliminate his critical judgments, and only relate "facts" to
"theories." Marcuse, the septuagenerian intellectual of the Movement,
has capped the criticisms of objectivity in his discussion of repressive
tolerance.[27] Perceiving objectivity as a derivative of the abstract conception of tolerance suitable to a true democracy, Marcuse points out that
in a "totalitarian democracy" in which effective dissent is stifled, such
even-handedness actually serves to silence critical thought and shore up
the holders of power. He writes:

This is prior to all expression and communication, a matter of semantics: the blocking of effective dissent, of the recognition of that which is not of the Establishment which begins in the language that is publicized and administered. The meaning of words is rigidly stabilized. Rational persuasion, persuasion to the opposite, is all but precluded. The avenues of entrance are closed to the meaning of words and ideas other than the established one—established by the publicity of the powers that be, and verified in their practices.[28]

The impartiality of the newscaster is an analogue of the objectivity of the social scientist and equally pernicious:

. . . if a newscaster reports the torture and murder of civil rights workers in the same unemotional tone he uses to describe the stock-market or the weather, or with the same great emotion with which he says his commercials, then such objectivity is spurious—more, it offends against humanity and truth by being calm where one should be enraged, by refraining from accusation where accusation is in the facts themselves. The tolerance expressed in such impartiality serves to minimize or even absolve prevailing intolerance and suppression.[29]

The university devoid of humane compassion has been described by a former graduate student of the political science department of the University of California:

. . . the routine life of the university is destructive of anything we know of educational tradition: especially at the level where we might reasonably expect to see painstaking efforts to give mass education its highest expression at your level as undergraduate. In the place of such efforts, your routine is comprised of a systematic psychological and spiritual brutality inflicted by a faculty of "well-meaning and nice" men who have decided that your situation is hopeless when it comes to actually participating in serious learning. . . . In the sciences and technical fields your courses are bluntly and destructively rigorous . . . you become impatient with "that" social sciences and humanities crap. . . . You perform. But when do you think?[30]

Another student writes of the effect of the "social aimlessness" of university administrators on students:

The effect of this social aimlessness on the individual students, particularly the undergraduate, is that the education he receives at Cal has very little relevance to his prospects in life and the

alternatives open to him. If survival and alienation are critical
problems to everybody including the student, why is not education aimed at uncovering the issues and explaining the alternatives? But this is not done, and the student's four-year-stay here
is painfully dull and frustrating. What makes that time tolerable
is the social and intellectual contacts with other students and
the promise of respectability and economic gain.[31]

And Mario Savio describes the University of California as producing
human resources for industry and the military but neglecting the humanities, the poor, and the despised:

Those disciplines with a ready market in industry and government are favored and fostered: the natural sciences, engineering,
mathematics, and the social sciences when these serve the brain-
trusting propaganda purposes of "liberal" government. The
humanities naturally suffer, so that what should be the sub-
stance of undergraduate education suffers. The emphasis is
given to research instead of to teaching undergraduates. . . .
But the undergraduate has become the new dispossessed; the
heart has been taken from his education—no less so for science
students—for the humanities are no longer accorded the central
role they deserve in the university.

And of course there are whole areas which never see the light
in undergraduate instruction. Who takes undergraduate courses
in the history of the labor movement, for example? Certainly
no one at the University of California. Likewise, American
Negro history is a rarity and is still more rarely taken seriously.
To be taken at all seriously it would have to be seen as central
to all American history.[32]

Existential Beliefs. The new humane compassion tends to perceive
American society as embracing two cultures. One is the culture of the
white middle class, composed of professional, managerial and service
personnel, and the unionized workers of industry—all of whom benefit
from the nation's affluence, support its domestic and foreign policies
within the framework of a two-party system, and feel a sense of frustration with or charity toward its poorer and deprived citizenry. The
other is composed of its poor, exploited, and proscribed classes, races,
and groups, including the ethnic minorities (i.e., Negroes, Orientals,
Mexican-Americans, Indians, and Puerto Ricans); the rural and urban
poor; and the less visible but nonetheless exploited and oppressed
groups—hippies, homosexuals, youth and students. The poor, the

young, the deviant, and the minorities constitute an under-class, a proletariat, whose common misery arises from the grinding oppression and poverty, the material and spiritual neglect, and the moral and cultural blindness of the more affluent and powerful groups.

In addition to its conception of a domestic proletariat, the Movement designates and identifies with certain of those peoples throughout the world who are victims of colonial domination, economic exploitation and national and cultural discrimination. Thus the oppressed African under white rule, the poverty-stricken Latin American peasant, and the Vietnamese national longing for self-determination are all objects of compassionate interest, material or moral aid, and personal and group identification. There are the beginnings of a conception of oppressed and exploited peoples everywhere sharing both a common misery and a common outlook. Comparisons between the ghettos of Black America and the hamlets of Vietnam are sometimes made, while the white suburbs of the United States and the skyscrapers of Saigon are also seen as serving a common function: temporarily protecting the rich and the white from an ever increasing revolutionary assault by oppressed and revolutionary elements.[33]

The Vietnamese War for national liberation, with its mixture of horror and heroism, and the Black Revolution, with its combination of radical rhetoric and redemptive reconstruction, are both cited and compared by movement leaders seeking to widen the blanket of compassion and revolt in the movement. "We are all the Viet Cong" is a slogan that at one and the same time forces the boundaries of humanity beyond the borders of America and suggests a revolutionary approach to social and political affairs. Furthermore such comparisons and slogans transform powerlessness into potency and convert the helpless into the strategic. Thus Ray Mungo, founder of the Liberation News Service, has written in response to Tom Hayden's assertion that "We are all the Viet Cong":

> And why not? Why not all the Vietcong, I asked myself. We know America because we live here, and we have a stake in its future. We are subject to tyranny like Diem's and to a "democratic process" which invests all power in a ruling elite who accept new recruits on their own terms only. We can, if we choose, mobilize our numbers to halt that machinery which is capable of mass murder—what's more important, we can do it when nobody else can. We can dump acid in the drinking water, refuse to pay our taxes, bomb our draft boards, clog the jails, register thousands of fraudulent subscriptions to hundreds of

book, record, and magazine clubs, close down Wall Street,
subvert the American army, take over the streets, stage music
festivals, tear down the slums and start all over. We can run the
places which we physically occupy: the universities, the ghettos,
the high schools, even the induction centers. And we already
have the beginnings of our counter-society; we have our own
presses, our own free schools, our own communes. We have
already broken away from the suffocation of mainstream America.[34]

If the existential beliefs of some members of the Movement conceive
of oppressed people everywhere as Viet Cong, still others wish to see
the students of America as no better than America's most despised
pariah caste. "Students are niggers," writes Jerry Farber, an instructor
at California State College at Los Angeles. "When you get that straight,
our schools begin to make sense."[35] Students, according to this view,
are victims of discrimination and oppression. They eat in separate
commons from faculty, vote in meaningless student body elections but
are denied franchise rights in matters of curricula, defer to faculty
administrators by employing an imposed obsequious rhetoric of subordination, and obey the most arbitrary and unreasonable instructions
of their hireling superiors, the professors. Further, students like Negro
slaves in America, respond to their situation either as "uncle toms,"
opportunists, or revolutionaries. The first are rewarded for their exem-
plary obedience; the second manipulate but do not undermine their
oppressors for short term advantages; and the third are punished by
suspension or expulsion. Most students accept the "system" for what
it is and either internalize its values, norms, and beliefs as their own
or exploit its weaknesses for gain or thrills. A few are serious enough
about education and troubled sufficiently about educational practices
to seek openly for change and reconstruction. The latter are severely
repressed, their lives and accomplishments maimed by punishments
imposed by a rigid and recalcitrant bureaucracy. But, so the argument
runs, students, recognizing their ignominious status as niggers, should
adopt the style and outlook of America's militant blacks. Therein lies
hidden power and true redemption:

> Students, like black people, have immense unused power. They
> could, theoretically, insist on participating in their own educa-
> tion. They could make academic freedom bilateral. They could
> teach their teachers to thrive on love and admiration, rather
> than fear and respect, and to lay down their weapons. Students
> could discover community. And they could learn to dance by

dancing on the IBM cards. They could make coloring books out of the catalogs and they could put the grading system in a museum. They could raze one set of walls and let life come blowing into the classroom. They could raze another set of walls and let education flow out and flood the streets. They could turn the classroom into where it's at—a "field of action" . . . . And, believe it or not, they could study eagerly and learn prodigiously for the best of all possible reasons—their own reasons.[36]

Still another student, moved by the new spirit of liberation on American university campuses, is disturbed by "the anomaly of our conservative tactics in the light of our radical goals." Stephen Saltonstall refutes the twin myths that change can only be brought about by actions taken within the framework of the democratic process and that civil disobedience and disruption alienate more people than they convert. Like those radical writers cited above, Saltonstall believes that much unutilized power resides among the supposedly powerless and that it should be employed immediately to end the Viet Nam war and to further enhance student power in the general polity as well. He writes:

I propose, then, that we seek to destroy the university's capacity to prop up our political institutions. By stalemating America's intellectual establishment, we may be able to paralyze the political establishment as well.

First we have the capability to immobilize the ROTC on the campuses. This would seriously affect the army's capacity to wage war, as more officers are turned out by the colleges than by the service academies, and there is already a serious shortage of second lieutenants in Vietnam. A small, disciplined group of "shock troops" could pack classes, break up drills, and harass army "professors."

Second, we can stop the defense research being carried on under university auspices. The Kissingers and Rostows should be locked, blocked from entering their offices, and harried at their homes. Students could infiltrate the office staffs of the electronic accelerators and foreign policy institutes, and hamper their efficiency. The introduction of a small quantity of LSD in only five or six government department coffee-urns might be a highly effective tactic. Students should prevent their universities from being used as forums for government apologists. Public figures like Humphrey and McNamara, when they appear, should be subject to intimidation and humiliation.

Finally, college administrations can be slowed to a near-standstill
if students overuse the bureaucracy. Floods of petitions can be
filed with deans and registrars. Appointments by the score can
be made with their assistants just for the hell of it. An inordinate
number of library books can be checked out. IBM cards can be
bent so they will be rejected by computers, and so forth.[37]

Normative Beliefs. The humane compassion of the Movement is
directed toward relief for the poor, the proscribed, and the oppressed.
The elimination of poverty, the abolition of stigmatized statuses, and
the equality of man are the most general features promised in the
utopia. However, it is important to note that self-determination, autonomy, and freedom rather than any system of benevolent but constricting beliefs are the primary goals of the Movement. Marcuse has pointed
out that the ethic of the new society will be aesthetic.

> The aesthetic as the possible Form of a free society appears at
> that stage of development where the intellectual and material
> resources for the conquest of scarcity are available, where previ-
> ously progressive repression turns into regressive suppression,
> where the higher culture in which the aesthetic values (and the
> aesthetic truth) had been monopolized and segregated from the
> reality collapses and dissolves in desublimated, "lower," and
> destructive forms, where the hatred of the young bursts into
> laughter and song, mixing the barricade and the dance floor,
> love play and heroism.[38]

The new society will employ the aesthetic dimensions as the criterion
by which freedom will be gauged. In such a society those persons and
groups who today arouse humane compassion would be liberated from
technological, social, and personal oppression.

> A universe of human relationships no longer mediated by the
> market, no longer based on competitive exploitation or terror,
> demands a sensitivity bred from the repressed satisfactions of
> the unfree societies; a sensitivity receptive to forms and modes
> of reality which thus far have been projected only by the
> aesthetic imagination. For the aesthetic needs have their own
> social content: they are the claims of the human organism, mind
> and body, for a dimension of fulfillment which can be created
> only in the struggle against the institutions which, by their very
> functioning, deny and violate these claims. . . . The aesthetic
> morality is the opposite of puritanism.[39]

The Movement will end the misery of the current objects of humane compassion by establishing a new order which not only eliminates the conditions of their misery but in the very process of that elimination liberates these and all other men according to the free prescriptions of a hitherto untried ethic—the aesthetic.

Relevance

The demand for relevance is a pervasive feature of the student movement. Relevance is the obverse side of meaninglessness and normlessness—twin features of the self-acknowledged alienation that enshrouds modern man. What is demanded here is that any mode of life that must be lived within the framework of an institutional setting be both understandable and significant to those who experience it. Meaningfulness must be experienced in knowledge that is related to decision-making, useful for social action, or evocative of a synthesis of passion and cognition.

Psychic meaningfulness is that which arises when reason and passion are simultaneously tapped and melded; when the senses are raised to an equal station with that of reason; when the person feels that his sensibilities are being both exercised and taken into account in the operation of any institution. The concept of the "whole person" is important here. Modern society, especially in its urban forms of social and personal organization, as sociologists such as Georg Simmel[40] and Louis Wirth[41] have observed, emphasizes the segmented self, depersonalized relationships, rational deliberation undertaken at the expense of passionate involvement, and a pervasive sense of lonely isolation. Only when the total person is restored to his rightful place in thought and society—when reason and passion are united and equalized—will the proper relationship between man and culture be established. What seems to be required ultimately is the establishment of a social system in which fundamentally new philosophical hedonism is the central value. Institutionalization of this hedonistic value orientation, especially in the arenas of knowledge and in socio-economic conditions, will end the current separation between a life of reason and one of pleasure. As Marcuse puts it:

> When knowledge of truth is no longer linked to knowledge of guilt, poverty, injustice, it is no longer forced to remain external to a happiness ceded to immediate sensual relationships. Even the most personal human relations can be opened to

happiness in a really guiltless knowledge. Perhaps they would thereby become, in fact, that free community in life of which idealist morality had expected the highest unfolding of individuality. Knowledge will no longer disturb pleasure, which the ancient idea of *nous* had dared to see as the highest determination of knowledge. . . . The development of material wants must go together with the development of psychic and mental wants. The organization of technology, science, and art changes with their changed utilization and changed content. When they are no longer under the compulsion of a system of production based on the unhappiness of the majority, and of the pressures of rationalization, internalization, and sublimation, then mind and spirit can only mean an augmentation of happiness. Hedonism is both abolished and preserved in critical theory and practice.[42]

A second sense of relevance is the demand that knowledge be related to life experiences. Ironically, this demand also has its "bourgeois" version in the demand, often heard in college courses with a heavy emphasis on theory, that the subject matter be more closely related to everyday practice. The question asked by a liberal arts major—"What job can I get out of it?"—reflects this narrow concern for a "rational" relationship between acquired knowledge and actual occupations. The current demand, however, expands the scope of relevance far beyond the relationship of knowing a subject to doing a job. Knowledge here is to be related to the broad range of human concerns—emotional, practical concerns—and also to the actual ways of life of those who learn. Moreover, the older conception of practical knowledge is sometimes rejected as debasing in itself, measuring the fullness of man merely by the breadth of his visible occupational achievements.

Finally, although knowledge is not solely to be utilized for pragmatic concerns, it should be employed to change society. The distinguishing point here is that practical knowledge rests on an implicit agreement with the existing order and an underlying contract to support that order. In contrast there is what might be called "utopian" knowledge— the treatment of learning for an open-ended world, a world subject to change by human activity, activity rooted in ideas that assume the relevance of man's thoughts and actions for social amelioration. Moreover, "utopian" knowledge requires that man not only rely on proven experiments but also that he dream of a future beyond the mere extrapolation of the present. "The fundamental change in our social system," writes Robert Theobald, "is from the past when it was necessary for man to continue to strive to achieve the power he needed to be able to create the environment he wanted, to the immediate future when it will be possible to do what men wish; but it will be essential to have the wisdom to know what man should wish for himself."[43]

Existential Beliefs. The theme of relevance is primarily one that arises in the colleges and universities. According to the Movement, higher education is devoted to irrelevant or pernicious research, deleterious to progressive social amelioration, and destructive of or detached from human values. Speaking of the modern university in America, Student Frederick Richman describes its characteristics as it developed from a place of cloistered learning to a handmaiden of the industrial order: "The University has become less a community of scholars and more a puberty rite and requirement for one's job resume." He continues:

> As the university has become democratic, it has incorporated more and more of the characteristics of the American demos, including the anti-intellectual strain that prefers action over thought, power over dialogue, practice over theory. Student activism is closely related to the tradition of American anti-intellectualism. Increasingly, today's students want to do something with their education, and they want to do it while they are in college. Their education gives them some understanding of society's problems, but little of the involvement that constitutes real awareness.[44]

Involvement and awareness are two central elements of relevance missing from current educational efforts. Not only students but also some professors have stated their agony over the current isolation of social knowledge from social affairs. Thus political scientist Robert Engler has written:

> What is the style and character of the knowledge being offered in the schools? Essentially marketable skills. Professors are experts who teach techniques, whether in economics, sociology, politics, or the behavioral sciences. Research is elevated as the ultimate goal. Amply footnoted platitudes elucidate the obvious. Isolated events are magnified out of all proportions to their value. Painstakingly gathered data are used to bring more clarity to subjects than may be inherent in them. Relationships not worth developing, but lending themselves to verification, are documented, while fundamental patterns of social structure remain obscure.[45]

In its concern for awareness and involvement the Movement emphasizes direct participation in the activities hitherto but dimly reflected

in academic study. True awareness has been at least partially achieved
in the sit-ins, freedom rides, demonstrations, and other civil rights and
anti-war activities, but the university fails to provide the moral equivalent of these. That sense of passionate commitment and unalloyed
understanding is yet to be achieved in the academy, and it cannot be
done by the traditional modes of listening to dull lectures and learning
"artificial" scientific methods.

Today, the best method of learning is, in the language of the more
drug-oriented realm of the Movement, to "tune in, turn on, and drop
out." Putting aside the middle term of that exhortation for the moment, we have here a claim that learning is achieved more by direct
experience than by secondary reading and vicarious association. Again
this view is also found among some professors. Analyzing the sociological classic *Street Corner Society*, Professor Richard R. Korn describes
its author as a thoughtful young man interested in social reform who
had to find out what was wrong both with himself and society.[46] "So,
anyway, instead of just *reading* about it—which is what you are doing—
he went and finessed the college treasury out of a lot of money, and
then he went into the slums of Boston. And just hung around. He
hung around the street corners for two solid years." But, as Korn
presents it, the university wasn't about to let out the secret that learning might be accomplished by direct experience with the subjects
under study:

> And then he came back to the university and wrote his book.
> And everybody was stoned clear out of their minds with it. And
> everybody—even some of the people who had seen a street-
> corner once—said, "Yeah, that's the way it is; he told it like it
> is." Even the professors said that. But the professors had a
> problem. What if every smart-ass kid got the same idea and
> dropped out of school in order to get an education? What would
> happen then?

The professors solved their problem by persuading the bright young
researcher that actually he did not "just go out and hang around the
street corner like some dumb-ass kid." No, he had engaged in *participant-observation*, a scientific procedure known to professional academics
and learned at universities. And so William Foote Whyte, the young
social scientist who had lived for two years in Boston's slums, wrote
an appendix to his study explaining how he had employed the method
known as participant-observation. "The kid was smart enough to figure
out that was the thing to do in order to get into the club. So now he's
a professor and a great authority on delinquency."

Moreover, Korn goes on, the university continues to engage in precisely this same conspiracy of silence against the real method of learning—direct experience. At the same time that they feel that their own perspectives as well as those of the dispossessed provide a clearer picture of social reality than those of their professors, the students sense a choking constriction on their sensibilities, a repression of their desires, and an unbearable slavery in irrelevant classes and assignments. The Free Speech Movement quoted with approving sympathy a letter written by a young girl. The girl is, according to her own statement, "a hard-working student in the oldest girls' school in the country." She loves her school, stays up doing her homework till past midnight, and has definite educational aspirations and a particular occupation in mind. But she is impatient, confused, and anxious:

Okay, I can wait. But meanwhile I'm wasting these years of preparation. I'm not learning what I want to learn. I don't care anymore whether $2 \times 2 = 4$ anymore. I don't care about the feudal system. I want to know about life. I want to think and read. When? Over weekends when there are projects and lectures and compositions, plus catching up on sleep.

My life is a whirlpool. I'm caught up in it but I'm not conscious of it. I'm what you call living, but somehow I can't find life. Days go by in an instant. So maybe I got an A on that composition I worked on for three hours, but when I get it back I find that A means nothing. It's a letter YOU use to keep me going.

Everyday I come in all prepared. Yet I dread every class; my stomach tightens and I sit tense. I drink coffee morning, noon, and night. At night, after my homework, I lie in bed and wonder if I've really done it all. Is there something I've forgotten?

At the beginning of the year I'm fine. My friends know me by my smile. Going to start out bright this year. Not going to get bogged down this year. Weeks later I become introspective and moody again. I wonder what I'm doing here. I feel phony; I don't belong. All I want is time; time to sit down and read what I want to read, and think what I want to think.

You wonder about juvenile delinquents. If I ever become one, I'll tell you why it will be so. I feel cramped. I feel like I'm in a coffin and can't move or breathe. There's no air or light. All I can see is blackness and I've got to burst. Sometimes I feel maybe something will come along. Something has to or I'm not worth anything. My life is worth nothing. It's enclosed in a few buildings on one campus; it goes no further. I've got to bust.[47]

An anonymous pamphlet written by FSM students observed that "This letter is probably one of the most profoundly shared expressions of anguish in American life today. It is shared by millions of us."[48]

Echoing similar sentiments, a graduate student at Princeton University wrote to George F. Kennan concerning the latter's plea that the university be restored as that quiet institution of learning and wisdom that was epitomized in the educational philosophy of Woodrow Wilson.[49] The student spoke of a "malaise that I have observed among graduate students," continuing:

> A university in our society is not the calm place that Wilson sought. When, for example, the experiment is not succeeding, it is not uncommon for the student to feel that he is not going anywhere and become discouraged and feel that he has been wasting his energy. To such a student it is a great relief to be able to do something "meaningful," like take part in a demonstration. Perhaps some also turn to drugs for a release from the sense of purposelessness.

However, as the student himself implies subsequently, the current malaise does not only affect the student temporarily disappointed with the progress of an experiment: "It was all right for a Medieval monk to spend his days copying illuminated manuscripts," he writes. "He was not pressed for time and his future, culminating in entrance to Heaven, was secure. But the graduate student in his moments of uncertainty knows that he will have to support a family someday and will have his employment chances impaired if he lacks the degree. In a Calvinist society, the pressure to achieve was bad enough but it did not have to coexist with a hedonism that stresses immediacy and a technology that renders the future problematical." Concluding his commentary, the Princetonian locates his own pessimistic position within the context of recent social philosophy:

> Ortega y Gasset saw the historical crisis of the post-Medieval world as finally ending with the emergence of modern rationalism, of Cartesian man. He suggested that the present period would ultimately give way to some new equilibrium. The way things are going, though, I find it difficult to detect any improvement in the essential quality of life in the foreseeable future. (Probably many who turn to drugs and/or political extremism also feel this way.) My great hope is that some people will find fulfillment by refusing to have the robots do everything for them and rediscovering artisan skills and the art

of tilling soil without the interference of machinery. But, alas, maybe this Tolstoyan Romanticism is just another form of extremism.

Normative Beliefs. The reestablishment of meaningful education in particular and a meaningful life in general is the utopian dream of the student radicals. Such a state would be realized when learning and life are not separated by an overbearing institutional or obtuse intellectual gulf, when the aim of learning is the realization of a truly authentic life, and when progressive reform rather than stultifying immobility animates the educational spirit.

The university might become the principal agency of social change. "I propose," writes Frederick Richman, "that the university become a political institution. . . Congress . . . possesses neither the time nor the expertise nor, apparently, the willingness to lead the country towards the social progress that invigorates a nation and keeps it alive." In place of Congress the "university might serve this function. People after 30 tend to retire into personal interests and private concerns. Students, however, have fewer private responsibilities and fewer commitments to established ways of living." Richman concludes:

> In the university of the future political activism, which the Greeks called citizenship, would be the central educational experience. The really important political developments would be taking place among youth. If someone wanted to see what was really going on politically in the country, he would look to the university to see what students were doing: there would be vastly increased numbers of them out working in society for various forms of social change or social progress.[50]

Professors sympathetic with some or all of the aims of the Movement have offered related, if more moderate, proposals to relieve students of the burdens arising from either the implacable supportive role the university plays with respect to industry and war, or of the unpromising future paraded by the end-of-ideology social sciences. Noam Chomsky writes:

> No one would seriously propose that the schools attempt to deal directly with such contemporary events as the American attack on the rural population of Vietnam or the backgrounds in recent history for the atrocities that are detailed in the mass media. But it is perhaps not ridiculous to propose that the schools might direct themselves to something more abstract, to an

attempt to offer students some means for defending themselves from the onslaught of the massive government propaganda apparatus, from the natural bias of the mass media, and . . . from the equally natural tendency of significant segments of the American intellectual community to offer their allegiance, not to truth and justice, but to power and the effective exercise of power.[51]

And in a reconceptualization of political science that sounds similar to the ideas of Lester F. Ward, Professor Christian Bay has observed:

My position is that the proper purpose of politics *is identical with the proper purpose of medicine: to postpone death and to reduce suffering.* Political science does not prescribe drugs, for its competence is not in human physiology or body chemistry; but it should aim at prescribing the organizational innovations and social experimentation that will allow us to cultivate, in Albert Schweitzer's term, a "reverence for life."[52]

A more specific demand for relevance and meaningfulness is expressed by militant black educators. Speaking of the black studies curricula developed by white professors, Nathan Hare asserts:[53]

With regard to course content, the white aim is mainly to black out the black perspective. White professors at universities such as Yale will dust off old courses in race relations and African tribalism for what might be called a polka-dot studies program, while Negro professors will trot out their old courses in Negro history and Negro music for Negro-studies courses which they cynically call black. If all a black-studies program needs is a professor with a black skin to prattle about Negro subject matter, then our Negro schools would never have failed so painfully as they have.

In contrast to assimilation-oriented "Negro" history and integration-oriented "Negro" sociology, Hare insists on the prior relevance of a nationalistic "black" history and a revolutionary "black" perspective:

In the search for educational relevance, black today is revolutionary and nationalistic. A black-studies program which is not revolutionary and nationalistic is, accordingly, quite profoundly irrelevant. The black revolutionary nationalist, aware and proud of his blackness, demands the right to exist as a distinct category, to be elevated as such by any means necessary. The Negro, contrarily would just as soon be white. He longs to escape his blackness and, in the search for integration achieves disintegration.

Hare goes on to urge the need for a special black perspective because "Black students are descendants of a people cut off from their attachment to land, culture and nation (or peoplehood)." Moreover, their education exacerbates their cultural alienation and produces a mortification of the ego in black children. A black perspective, by contrast, "can restore and construct a sense of pastness, of collective destiny, and further it could act as a springboard to the quest for a new collective future. For black children crippled by defeatist attitudes, hardened by generations of exclusion, this is potentially therapeutic." But beyond its peculiar perspective and therapeutic value, black studies must have a pragmatic component "which focuses on the applied fields of knowledge such as economics." Hare concludes by describing how the "pure" sciences might be harnessed to positive programs of black liberation and community uplift:

> Many will argue that science and mathematics are "pure" subjects; though that may be true in a sense, the uses of science may be directed toward atomic weapons of destruction, or in the case of a community-oriented black studies, devoted to such matters as rat control. I can visualize, for instance, a reading program in "black" mathematics that would not be saturated with middle-class referents such as stocks and bonds. Rather, the teacher might ask in order to whet the ghetto child's appetite for math: "If you loot one store and burn two, how many do you have left?" The example might be improved; but there is no substitute for a black perspective based on the principle of self-control.

Paul Goodman has addressed himself to another element of change desirable in higher education: the broadening of academic freedom to include the idea of *Lernfreiheit* as well as *Lehrfreiheit*. The latter concept refers to the freedom of professors to teach according to their own beliefs, the more traditional concept of academic freedom. *Lernfreiheit*, on the other hand, refers to the rights of students to regulate their own education in terms of fields of study, choice of teachers, sequence of learning, and so on. The right is already known in the historical tradition of European and Latin education. *Lernfreiheit* "goes with early sexual maturity, with economic independence (often in bohemian poverty), and with active involvement in politics. Classically, in Europe, it has also involved drawn-out education, many moratoria, much changing of schools and career plans, and 'being a student' as itself a kind of profession of young adults, especially of the upper class."[54] As Goodman points out, these concomitant characteristics are already present in America.

One kind of meaningfulness that the students have in mind is realized in the "communes" which have been established in the buildings occupied during student demonstrations. Writing of the communes established during the Columbia demonstrations of 1968, Mark Rudd explained:

> The communes were the locus of political power. This was one of the first times in our experience that "participatory democracy" had been put into practice. Questions such as negotiations, the demands, whether to resist the cops, the goals of the strike, the goals of the movement were debated fully by nearly everyone in the commune. The original Strike Coordinating Committee had an understanding that no major policy could be changed or initiated unless each of the four liberated buildings agreed. That meant hours, even full days, before decisions could be made. It also meant intense discussion, sometimes lasting as long as twelve hours, in which people participated and grew in their political understanding.[55]

Another kind of relevance is derivative from the special form of hedonism—"gamesmanship"—advocated as both a reconceptualization of everyday affairs and as a new style of life by Timothy Leary:

> Those of us who talk and write about the games of life are invariably misunderstood. We are seen as frivolous or cynical anarchists tearing down the social structure. This is an unfortunate misapprehension. Actually, only those who see culture as a game, only those who take this evolutionary point of view, can appreciate and treasure the exquisitely complex magnificence of what human beings do and have done. To see it all as "serious, taken-for-granted reality" is to miss the point; is to derogate with bland passivity the greatness of the games we learn.
>
> Those of us who play the game of "applied mysticism" respect and support good gamesmanship. You pick out your game. You learn the rules, rituals, concepts. You play fairly and cleanly. You don't confuse your games with other games. You win today's game with humility. You lose tomorrow's game with dignity. Anger and anxiety are irrelevant because you see your small

game in the context of the great evolutionary game which no one can win, no one can lose.[56]

However the good life may be conceived—as a game, as intimately involved with humanity, as evoking the perfect synthesis of reason and passion—the members of the Movement appear to agree that it is realized in positive experience, in action. And our next concern will be the relation between this action and the persistence of the ideology.

Notes

[1]The joint theme of alienation and the quest for community is perceptively examined by Robert A. Nisbet, *Community and Power* (New York: Oxford Galaxy, 1962).

[2]C. Wright Mills, *The Power Elite* (New York: Oxford Galaxy, 1956).

[3]*Ibid.*, p. 361. For a thoughtful critique of Mills' position, see Talcott Parsons, "The Distribution of Power in American Society," in *Structure and Process in Modern Society* (Glencoe: The Free Press, 1960), pp. 199-225.

[4]Erich Fromm, *Escape from Freedom* (New York: Rinehart and Co., 1941), pp. 28-32.

[5]*Ibid.*, pp. 74-94, 130-31.

[6]Erich Fromm, "Psychoanalysis and Zen Buddhism," in *Zen Buddhism and Psychoanalysis*, eds. D. T. Suzuki, et al. (New York: Harper, 1960), pp. 77-142.

[7]*Ibid.*, p. 98.

[8]*Loc. cit.*

[9]John H. Schaar, *Escape from Authority* (New York: Basic Books, 1961), p. 311.

[10]For the use of paired concepts in sociology, see Reinhard Bendix and Bennett Berger, "Images of Society and Problems of Concept Formation in Sociology," in *Symposium on Sociological Theory*, ed. Llewellyn Gross (Evanston: Row, Peterson, 1959), pp. 92-120.

[11]William H. Whyte, *The Organization Man* (Garden City: Doubleday Anchor, 1956), pp. 449-56.

[12]"The Port Huron Statement," written primarily by Tom Hayden, was the originating manifesto of the Students for a Democratic Society (SDS) at their 1962 convention. At this convention SDS broke away from the League for Industrial Democracy, the parent organization from which SDS had been formed in 1960. The "Statement" is reprinted in Paul Jacobs and Saul Landau, eds., *The New Radicals* (New York: Vintage, 1966), pp. 149-62.

[13]Herbert Marcuse, *One-Dimensional Man* (New York: Beacon Books, 1968); Paul Goodman, *Growing Up Absurd* (New York: Vintage, 1962); Staughton Lynd, "History: Historical Past and Existential Present," in *The Dissenting Academy*, ed. Theodore Roszak (New York: Pantheon Books, 1967), pp. 92-109.

[14]Frantz Fanon, *The Wretched of the Earth* (New York: Grove Press, 1963); *Studies in a Dying Colonialism* (New York: Monthly Review Press, 1965); *Black Skin, White Masks* (New York: Grove Press, 1967); and *Toward the African Revolution* (New York: Monthly Review Press, 1967). For Malcolm X, see *The Autobiography of Malcolm X* (New York: Grove Press, 1964); *Malcolm X Speaks*

(New York: Merit Publishers, 1965); *The Speeches of Malcolm X at Harvard* (New York: William Morrow, 1968). For Martin Luther King, Jr., see *Stride Toward Freedom* (New York: Ballantine, 1958); *Why We Can't Wait* (New York: Signet, 1963); *Where Do We Go From Here* (New York: Harper and Row, 1967). For Che Guevara, see *The Diary of Che Guevara* (New York: Bantam Books, 1968); *Guerilla Warfare* (New York: Vintage, 1968); *Che Guevara Speaks* (New York: Merit Books, 1967).

[15]For Tom Hayden see the "Port Huron Statement," op. cit., and *Rebellion in Newark: Official Violence and Ghetto Response* (New York: Vintage, 1967). For Jerry Rubin see "An Emergency Letter to My Brothers and Sisters in the Movement," *New York Review of Books*, XII, No. 3 (February 13, 1969), 27-29. Abbie Hoffman has written a revolutionary tract under the pseudonym Free, *Revolution for the Hell of It* (New York: The Dial Press, Inc., 1968). See Mark Rudd, "Symbols of the Revolution," in Jerry L. Alvorn, et al., *Up Against the Ivy Wall* (New York: Atheneum, 1968); and Mario Savio, "An End to History," in Hal Draper, *Berkeley: The New Student Revolt* (New York: Grove Press, Inc., 1965), pp. 179-82; and "The Berkeley Student Rebellion of 1964," in *The Free Speech Movement and the Negro Revolution* (Detroit: News and Letters, 1965), pp. 15-19; Stokely Carmichael and Charles V. Hamilton, *Black Power: The Politics of Liberation in America* (New York: Vintage Books, 1967); Nathan Hare, *The Black Anglo-Saxons* (New York: Marzane and Munsell, 1965); "How White Power Whitewashes Black Power," in *The Black Power Revolt*, ed. Floyd B. Barbour (Boston: Extending Horizons Books, Porter Sargent, 1968), pp. 182-88; and "The Case for Separatism: 'Black Perspective,' " *Newsweek* (February 10, 1969), p. 58; Daniel and Gabriel Cohn-Bendit, *Obsolete Communism: The Left Wing Alternative*, trans. Arnold Pomerans (New York: McGraw-Hill, 1968).

[16]See Talcott Parsons, "The Role of Ideas in Social Action," in *Essays in Sociological Theory* (New York: The Free Press of Glencoe, 1964), pp. 19-33.

[17]*Ibid.*

[18]The following quotes are taken from the "Statement" appearing in Jacobs and Landau, op. cit.

[19]Parsons, "The Role of Ideas in Social Action," op. cit.

[20]Jacobs and Landau, op. cit., p. 4.

[21]See Steve Weissman, "Freedom and the University," in Jacobs and Landau, *ibid.*, pp. 234-37.

[22]For a discussion of the underlying theory of these modes of therapy see Carl R. Rogers, "The Characteristics of a Helping Relationship," in *Interpersonal Dynamics: Essays and Readings on Human Interaction*, Revised Edition, eds. Warren G. Bennis, et al. (Homewood, Ill.: The Dorsey Press, 1968), pp. 287-303; Rogers, "The Therapeutic Relationship: Recent Theory and Research," in *The Human Dialogue: Perspectives on Communication*, eds. Floyd W. Matson and Ashley Montagu (New York: The Free Press of Glencoe, 1967), pp. 246-59; J. F. T. Bugental and Robert Tannenbaum, "Sensitivity Training and Being Motivation," in *Sociology in Action: Case Studies in Social Problems and Directed Social Change*, ed. Arthur B. Shostak (Homewood, Ill.: The Dorsey Press, 1966), pp. 82-92.

[23]Louis Wirth, "The Problem of Minority Groups," in *The Science of Man in the World Crisis*, ed. Ralph Linton (New York: Columbia University Press, 1946), p. 364.

[24]Free (pseud. for Abbie Hoffman), op. cit., p. 157.

[25]Carey McWilliams, "Foreword," in *The New Student Left*, eds. Mitchell Cohen and Dennis Hale (Boston: Beacon Press, 1966), p. vii.

[26]See Lester F. Ward, *The Psychic Factors of Civilization* (Boston: Ginn and Co., 1906), pp. 237-331; *Applied Sociology* (Boston: Ginn and Co., 1906).

[27]Herbert Marcuse, "Repressive Tolerance," in Robert P. Wolff, Barrington Moore, and Herbert Marcuse, A Critique of Pure Tolerance (Boston: Beacon Press, 1969), pp. 81-123.

[28]Ibid., pp. 95-96.

[29]Ibid., p. 98.

[30]Bradford Cleaveleand, "A Letter to Undergraduates," Slate Supplement Report I, 4 (September, 1964). Reprinted in The Berkeley Student Revolt, op. cit., pp. 66-81. Quotation from pp. 67-68.

[31]Richard Fallenbaum, "University Abdicates Social Responsibility," The Cal Reporter, May 13, 1963. Reprinted in ibid., pp. 64-66.

[32]Mario Savio, "The Berkeley Student Rebellion of 1964," The Free Speech Movement and the Negro Revolution, op. cit., pp. 17-18.

[33]See Howard Perdue and Tony Lobay, "Black Revolution and the N. L. F.—an Interview with H. Franz Schurmann," The Bowditch Review (Spring, 1968), pp. 37-48.

[34]Quoted in Ray Mungo, "From Bratislava to Washington," ibid., p. 34.

[35]Jerry Farber, "The Student as Nigger," in The Hippie Papers (New York: Signet Books, 1968), pp. 160-68.

[36]Loc. cit.

[37]Stephen Saltonstall, "Student Power: Toward a Strategy of Disruption," in The Hippie Papers, op. cit., p. 174.

[38]Herbert Marcuse, An Essay on Liberation (Boston: Beacon Press, 1969), pp. 25-26.

[39]Ibid., pp. 27-28.

[40]Georg Simmel, "The Metropolis and Mental Life," in The Sociology of Georg Simmel, ed. and trans. Kurt H. Wolff (Glencoe: The Free Press, 1950), pp. 409-26.

[41]Louis Wirth, "Urbanism as a Way of Life," American Journal of Sociology, XLIV (July, 1938), 1-24.

[42]Herbert Marcuse, "On Hedonism," Negations (Boston: Beacon Press, 1968), pp. 198-99.

[43]Robert Theobald, An Alternative Future for America (Chicago: The Swallow Press, 1968), p. 24.

[44]Frederick Richman, "The Disfranchised Majority," in Students and Society, op. cit., p. 5.

[45]Robert Engler, "Social Science and Social Consciousness," in The Dissenting Academy, ed. Theodore Roszak (New York: Pantheon Books, 1967), pp. 193-94.

[46]The following is from Richard R. Korn, ed., Juvenile Delinquency (New York: Thomas Y. Crowell, 1968), pp. 109-11.

[47]"We Want a University," in Draper, op. cit., pp. 192-93.

[48]Ibid., p. 193.

[49]The following quotes are taken from George F. Kennan, Democracy and the Student Left (New York: Bantam Books, 1968), pp. 27-33.

[50]Richman, "The Disenfranchised Majority," op. cit., pp. 5-6.

[51]Noam Chomsky, American Power and the New Mandarins (New York: Pantheon Books, 1967), pp. 313-14.

[52]Christian Bay, "Social Science: The Cheerful Science of Dismal Politics," in The Dissenting Academy, op. cit., pp. 225-26. Emphasis in original.

[53]The following is from Nathan Hare, "The Case for Separatism," Newsweek LXXIII (February 10, 1969), p. 56.

[54]Paul Goodman, "Thoughts on Berkeley," in *Beyond Berkeley*, eds. Christopher G. Katope and Paul G. Zolbrod (Cleveland, Ohio: World Publishing Co., 1966), p. 79.

[55]Mark Rudd, "Symbols of the Revolution," in *Up Against the Ivy Wall*, op. cit., pp. 294-95.

[56]Timothy Leary, "How to Change Behavior," in *Interpersonal Dynamics*, eds. Warren G. Bennis, et al. (Homewood, Ill.: Dorsey Press, 1968), p. 440.

Chapter IV
Problems
of Persistence

Sociological explanations traditionally focus on either causes or continuities. We have already dealt with the more general causes of student revolt and the nature of its supporting ideology. Now we are concerned with continuities.

Two sets of problems face us here. One has to do with questions concerning the persistence of the ideological belief system; the other, with questions concerning the activities themselves. Quite clearly, as we have already suggested, there exists dynamic feedback between beliefs and activities. But here we separate analytically the two problems to deal first with the mechanisms that facilitate the belief system and then with the game-generated fun that motivates persistence of action.

the Persistence
of Ideology

Five mechanisms have been identified by which persons maintain a belief system in the face of competing beliefs and repressive forces.[1] These are (1) selective attention; (2)

active structuring of situations; (3) unilateral interpretation of ambiguous evidence; (4) differential associations and identifications; and (5) comprehension and structuring of the larger society's ambivalence toward one's beliefs. All five of these mechanisms are at work within the student revolt. Although in their actual expression they are often overlapping and usually undifferentiated, it is useful to distinguish them analytically and to point out the special characteristics of each.

Selective Attention

Individuals choose from among the totality of incoming perceptions those that are congruent with or supportive of their already developed beliefs and expectations. This act itself is by no means simple. It includes a discrimination among objects competing for interpretive attention, an interpretive transformation of these objects into an event, and a connection of these events to an already established definition of the situation.

This selective process is nicely illustrated in the students' interpretations supporting the contention that universities are a central cog in the military-industrial complex that directs national policies toward imperialism abroad and the maintenance of repressive institutional controls at home. To clarify the point, consider three elements of perception: the presence of the police on campus, the government-sponsored contract research undertaken by universities, and the racial policies of university administrations.

When students deliberately hold a rally after authorization for it has been denied, when they forcibly occupy a building to establish an area liberated from oppressive dictates, or when young people take over a privately owned lot to establish a recreational park in defiance of public rules of property management, they put themselves in jeopardy of police action. Municipal or university authorities may attempt to justify their decision to use the police, but to no avail. The very fact of their employment is regarded by students and their compatriots as a betrayal of trust, a violation of the appropriate sense of community that should prevail on a campus, and ultimately as proof of the charges that the students have made against college and society.

Once a confrontation between police and students has occurred, the processes of selective attention operate to sustain opposed ideologies. University administrators, city mayors, chiefs of police, and state governors emphasize the "facts" that the situation was out of control; that mob violence threatened public order and private property; that a small group of radical agitators—perhaps secretly subsidized by alien or subversive elements—had taken advantage of genuine student grievances to further ulterior aims; and that real or potential civilian and police casualties required the use of force to defend society and repress unlawful violence. At the same time revolutionary leaders and sympathetic reporters point out that no effective negotiations over outstanding grievances were ever seriously entertained by the authorities; that a demonstration in behalf of their complaints was the students' only available choice; that the demonstrators were frivolous but not intending to initiate violence; that the police escalated the seriousness of the situation by their hostile reactions and brutal overreactions; and that except for police-inflicted wounds, little real injury did occur (and some of that was "trumped up" by the police themselves).

A second illustration of the selective interpretive process is drawn from the student perception of the military-industrial complex and its putative connection with the university.

A university is many things and its diversity of activity makes it difficult to describe and define simply. Student revolutionaries, however, have defined its *real* nature by pointing to the involvement of the university with the makers of munitions, the purveyors of pollutants, and the dealers in death. The ascetic scholarship of the classicist, the brilliant lectures of the historian, the melioristic intonations of the sociologist are all disattended and converted into irrelevant features—as irrelevant as the vase of flowers on the table beside a chess board when one is engrossed in that game. The student revolutionaries point out that the *significant* university is found in the laboratories where scientists spend their time studying methods of defoliation, and atomic, biological, and chemical warfare; and in the proliferating institutes of social and behavioral sciences, where scholars study counter-revolutionary strategy, provide psychological tools for "cooling out" the grievances of disgruntled citizenry, and spin out theories of utopia that manage to equate the *status quo* with perfected society. The revolutionary students "expose" the university by lifting the veil that hides its real purpose: to serve the interests of the power elite, to transform creative intelligence into acquiescent societal service, and to maintain the current social structure in its present form.

Radical students, then, perceive the university as engaged in a great conspiracy against progress and youth, in a great combine with elements of industry, labor, and government to further oppressive interests already established. What is significant is that this conspiracy can be perceived—whereas the nameless, impersonal monolithic power that supposedly commands their obedience and determines their destiny remains, for the students, real but unperceived. Like the Calvinists who converted the unperceived truth of God's will to the perceived truth of man's labor in a calling,[2] the radical students convert the unperceived truth of the actual state of oligarchical power in presumably democratic America to the perceived truth of university involvement in the military-industrial complex. And, for the radical students (our modern-day Calvinists), "grace" may be obtained by withholding complicity in its activities.

Similarly, the radical students perceive a racist conspiracy in the educational system. First, they point to a public educational system that demoralizes minorities and then excludes them from universities on the "reasonable" grounds of educational deficiency. Second, they note that the personnel in charge of admissions, scholarships, guidance, and placement are drawn largely from among the ranks of white people. Finally, they observe that the curriculum seems especially designed to emphasize white supremacy by systematically omitting mention of the histories, cultures, activities, and contributions of non-whites. Thus, they conclude the university is engaged in "institutional racism," far more subtle, much less visible than the simple prejudices of ordinary men or the gross discriminations in housing and jobs. This institutional racism goes unnoticed by ordinary white students until its manifestations and routines are sharply outlined by the protests of minorities and radicals.

Active Structuring of Social Situations

Defining a social situation may involve more than pure cognition, selective perception, and perceptual omissions. It can also include active intervention in the social arena creating the conditions of the very definition held. As Robert K. Merton once observed, if people believe a bank failure is imminent and rush to remove their savings, they create the very situation that they predicted.[3] Similarly, if students define the university as an active agent in support of the military-industrial complex, a conscious perpetrator of racist practices, and an ever-watchful instrument for the oppression of dissenters and radicals, and if in consequence of their beliefs they combine to prevent job interviews from chemical corporations, take-over the offices of the registrar, or obstruct the routine activities of the university in general, they are likely to be met with police restraint "proving" that the university is just as reprehensible as they originally argued.

Another point must be made concerning the intentions of students and others involved in demonstrations. To the cursory observer it might appear that virtually all the activists are fully committed to an ideology of revolution. But closer observation will show that the current youth movement is quite heterogeneous in composition and commitment. Radical students as individuals show considerable variation in their personal make-up and exhibit a good deal of uncertainty with respect to the publicly claimed righteousness of elements in their ideology and conduct.[4]

People will often engage in acts that they don't want to perform because, as members of a group, they each behave in terms of what they think others expect them to do. Rather than being hard-core members of a dedicated tight communion, persons find themselves caught up in radicalized situations. Once involved in such situations, they infer commitment to the common purpose by their reading of clues and cues, jokes and gestures, and barbs and banter that occur in interaction with others similarly situated. This phenomenon is by no means unique to student radical movements. The same mechanism has been discovered to operate among middle-class college youth who indirectly and unintentionally talk one another into committing robbery,[5] and among delinquents who, while never airing precisely their commitment to criminal codes of conduct, do nevertheless inadvertently lead their fellows into believing that their subculture is committed to delinquency by converting all questions on the subject into moral tests of masculinity for the interrogator.[6]

Anxieties and uncertainties arise among those involved in racial situations with respect to role, personal identity and reference group. Consider the case of a San Francisco State professor who found himself reflecting on his own student days and his subsequent conventional professional career: "I was a good boy in the academy, a graduate of Harvard, I even wrote three books, always a good academic boy." Then the force of events carried him into the fray, providing him with an opportunity to relive his past in the present, carve out a new identity that would expiate the sins of the old, and experience the catharsis of moral rebirth:

> One day, the Hayakawa loudspeakers were blaring that this was an illegal strike and two big black boys hoistered me up on their shoulders, and I spoke. You know the feeling, the adrenalin pours into you, the beautiful feeling. I addressed the crowd and did very well. Then I went to a faculty senate meeting and they were just talking and I left that . . . I walked to the stacks to look for a book and I just started to cry. I remembered the times when the part of me that I admired—I am some part a

private man, things I liked about myself, the quiet hours of lonely writing. I cried for that part. . . .

After that the professor joined the strike, marching in the picket line with a red arm band until the end. Without having articulated an ideology, he had experienced a sense of commitment and found a new peer group: "I know only," he reports, "that if I had refused to join the strike, I would have no right to teach in the classroom. . . . It seems strange to say this, but I like my students better than my colleagues. This is *life*."[7]

In a radicalized situation, the activities of some serve as models and moral challenges to others. Moreover, there is a reciprocating process of action, observation, and cooperative reaction in which each participant serves as mirror and monitor for the other. Formal leaders and charismatic figures who assume extreme positions and adopt bizarre postures serve as the measure of commitment to less committed others on the scene. Persons who had carefully planned only a limited participation in a confrontation find themselves drawn to escalate their activity in the light of immediate events and sudden challenges to morality. Thus Noam Chomsky, the distinguished linguist, reports on how his intentions to witness but not participate in civil disobedience during demonstrations at the Justice Department and Pentagon metamorphosed into activity leading to his arrest:

> I had decided not to take part in civil disobedience, and I do not know what in detail had been planned. As everyone must realize, it is very hard to distinguish rationalization from rationality in such matters. I felt, however, that the first large-scale acts of civil disobedience should be more specifically defined, more clearly in support of those who are refusing to serve in Vietnam, on whom the real burden of dissent must fall. . . . In any event, what actually happened was rather different from what anyone had anticipated. . . . The advancing line of soldiers had partially scattered the small group that had come with Dellinger. Those of us who had been left behind the line of soldiers regrouped, and Dr. Spock began to speak. Almost at once, another line of soldiers emerged from somewhere, this time in a tightly massed formation, rifles in hand, and moved slowly forward. We sat down. As I mentioned earlier, I had no intention of taking part in any act of civil disobedience, until that moment. But when that grotesque organism began slowly advancing—more grotesque because its cells were recognizable human beings—it became obvious that one could not permit that thing to dictate what one was going to do. I was arrested at that point by a federal marshal. . . .[8]

Still another point must be made in this respect. The debate and activities that are routine parts of campus revolts are moral tests for the participants. One element of the test is poise under pressure or what in modern parlance is called "keeping one's cool." Poise here refers to the capacity to execute physical tasks including speech and body idiom in a concerted, smooth and self-controlled manner under circumstances where that manner is challenged by composure-shattering elements of the immediate scene.[9] In the case of the current movement its ideology of personal freedom insures that there will be bizarre and shocking public displays during the course of political demonstrations. Thus the Free Speech Movement at the University of California was interrupted and its members temporarily disorganized and immobilized when a lone individual appeared at the campus with an obscene poster. A new interpretation of freedom of speech was hotly debated amid charges that the movement had become one favoring "filthy" as well as "free" speech and counter-charges that enemies had injected a spurious issue of "porno-politics." For the individuals involved, the moral test was whether their own libertarianism included public usages of taboo terms. Those who exhibited signs of shock or disgust were vulnerable to attacks on their real commitment to freedom.

In the rush of events since 1964 there has been an escalation of public displays that would ordinarily be shocking and presumably a growing inurement to displays of surprise, alarm, or outrage by members of the movement. Thus obscene language, nudity, sexual promiscuity, open use of drugs, exotic body decorations, and extraordinary clothing styles are prominent elements of current demonstrations. There would even appear to be an escalation of these elements as older forms become acceptable, thus continuing to put pressure on members of the movement to exhibit those characteristics of *savoir-faire* which Simmel at one time attributed to the urbanite and which are in fact characteristics associated wherever there is risk. Maintaining one's "cool" in the face of the barrage of bizarre sights and sounds is a permanent challenge provided by the current revolt.

Interpretation
of Ambiguous
Evidence

The ideology of the revolt and the counter-ideology of those who oppose it are both sustained in part by mutually opposed interpretations of ambiguous evidence in the mass media. For the Establishment and its supporters the reports of student conduct emphasize rude, vulgar, and outrageous conduct—unclean bodies, unkempt appearances, and unhealthy practices. The students are "shown" to have engaged in a betrayal of that trust which the community had taken for granted as a sign of ordinary moral beings. Thus when students display an open disregard for just those elements of morality and custom that the middle classes assume to be normal—when they seem to show contempt for the fundamental elements of public decency by tearing down the traditional separation of sexes in the public toilets of "liberated" buildings; when they seem to show a reckless disregard for human life by carrying and threatening to use guns and knives; when they seem to show no respect for privacy by rifling through the private files in university presidents' desks—the Establishment media point out that these activities are "proof" that the students are irrational, unreasonable, or disreputable.

At the same time, students and others in revolt point to the increasingly blurred distinction between the police and the military, the economic interests of the members of university boards of trustees, and the compromising rhetoric and practices of liberals to "prove" that there not only is an interlocking Establishment of political, military, industrial, labor, and educational leaders, but also that the Establishment is oppressive, vindictive, and dictatorial. Thus the offer of negotiations over heated issues—such as a "people's park"—are suspect and carefully scrutinized for hidden meanings and evil motives. In one not untypical instance Art Goldberg, commenting on the unsuccessful negotiations over Berkeley's "people's park" imbroglio observed: "The only reason they want to negotiate is to get people out of the streets."[10] Similarly, Thomas Hayden has pointed out that accession to power in university councils is not really an acceptable offer even when made by administrative officials. Admission of students to the education power structure is only acceptable "if their inclusion is a step toward transforming the university." Any other elevation of students to decision-making positions would be mere "cooptation"—a sham, hypocritical mode of maintaining the *status quo*. Students, concludes Hayden, "want a new and independent university standing against the mainstream of American society, or they want no university at all. They are, in Fidel Castro's words 'guerillas in the field of culture.' "[11]

The point here is this: All evidence is ambiguous and capable of multiple interpretations. Precisely because of this, situations charged with conflict, emotion, and ideologies are fraught with the possibilities for selective attention, mutually opposed definitions, and reinforcement of ideologies. Each side can point with pride to just those events that show itself to be virtuous, its enemies perfidious. Each side can point with painful justification to those words and deeds that demonstrate that the other side is as reprehensible as it has originally charged. Each side can point with scorn to the other side's selective distortion of its own activities. Ambiguities are real but in times of struggle, they are not permitted to survive as such.

Differential Association
and Identification

Typical of radical movements,[12] the current campus revolutionaries strive for seclusion from those outside sources of contact and communication that might sully the purity of their own beliefs, provide countervailing ideas and practices, and winnow out special elements of the ideology for criticism. As Weber seems to suggest in his discussion of prophecy, what is required in any revolutionary movement—whether religious or political—is a unified world view formed from a consciously meaningful orientation toward the world and realized in everyday attitudes and practical conduct.[13] Now when that orientation is at variance with conventionally held attitudes and rules of conduct, isolation and in-group identification are required for ideological maintenance and reinforcement. When ecological niches can be carved out of social space, private arenas of secluded communication and social solidarity fashioned from free areas, territories for recognition and response constructed on the public lands, the chances for ideological maintenance and group solidarity are increased. Just as the factory town presumably provided the appropriate enclave for the development of class solidarity among nineteenth-century workers because it isolated them from bourgeois influences and reinforced their consciousness of common membership,[14] so certain university towns, urban ghettos and bohemian settlements provide the opportunities for physical concentration, easy communication, and communal solidarity among youth in revolt.

Although campus revolts are widespread they tend to re-occur in certain locales. San Francisco, Berkeley, and New York are especially prominent in the current revolts. Each of these cities is a Mecca and haven for disillusioned youth, whether of the hippie or activist persuasion. In each of these cities there are considerable minority communities congregated in exclusive ghettos. Finally each of these cities has been the scene for the establishment of "home territories" among the newly disenchanted.[15] Greenwich Village in New York City, the Haight-Ashbury district in San Francisco, and Telegraph Avenue in Berkeley are each arenas in which the hippies and the activists, the dropouts and the disillusioned, and the "heads" and the "seekers"[16] may congregate and exchange ideas, information, and plans in relative isolation from intrusive elements of the larger society. Moreover, once these areas and the campuses associated with them become known as centers of youth in revolt, still more people disgusted with the present order, detached from social moorings, and deprived of a sense of community, flock to them to join their fellows in retreat and revolt. Finally, in each of these cities, and elsewhere, a flourishing underground press provides news, information, and editorial opinion in support of the ideology of unrest. Thus in territory, communicative media, and concentration the ideology is preserved, modified, and practiced. The practical world view of the ideology becomes an everyday affair in the lives of those who read the *Berkeley Barb*, reside in "pads" in the Telegraph Avenue or Haight-Ashbury districts, and "rap" with one another on both the mundane and major issues of life.

Within the enclaves of alienation and revolt that grow up around certain campuses a contraculture develops. This contraculture, although regarding traditional academic pursuits and the pressures of pre-professional training as irrelevant or enervating, is not entirely anti-intellectual. In its more sophisticated forms it finds its expression in what Kenneth Keniston calls "student existentialism"—"an intense interest in existential writers, in the theater of the absurd, and in philosophies and psychologists who stress 'existential' concepts."[17] Its less intellectual forms find expression in the exhortations in behalf of interpersonal honesty, being oneself, and an especially prominent presentation of open and disinterested authenticity in all encounters. Outside the environs of the contraculture, life is imagined to be fraudulent, exploitative, and unauthentic. Outside the environs of the disenchanted youth in revolt, people live according to hated "roles" in which they must adjust, and "play games" in order to survive. Those students and their compatriots who have joined the retreat from or the revolt against conventional society find a powerful aid in the counter-culture that has arisen in the new "ghettos" around the campuses. "Participation in this counter-culture," concludes Keniston, "provides a powerful support for efforts to explore oneself, to intensify relationships with other people, to change the quality and content of consciousness."[18]

Surrounded by conventional society, harassed by police and other officials, victimized by the operations of the military draft, and troubled by shortages of food, clothing, and drugs, the already alienated and disenchanted students develop the mentality appropriate to an oppressed minority. Certain elements among the students are members of well-established minorities—blacks, Indians, Mexican-Americans, etc.—and the others not infrequently adopt the style and rhetoric of these groups in self-conscious emulation. Whites dress in imitation of the

American Indian, students define themselves as "niggers," and Negroes struggle to become rebellious "blacks." Finally, there develops a private language and special argot that defines the peculiar experiences and special feelings of their members. The special language has another function, namely, that of providing legitimations for deviant and disapproved activities. We shall return to this crucial dimension of language in ideology shortly.

Ambivalence
of the Larger Culture

Although functionalist theory assumes the existence of a single overarching value consensus in any social system, it becomes apparent upon sober reflection or serious examination that the society built upon uniform consensus is but an existential possibility, and, considering the heterogeneity of peoples, races, religions, and classes, an unlikely possibility at that. A more fruitful model for the understanding of society is one that assumes plural value systems to be operating in a social arena characterized by competition, conflict, and precarious accommodation.[19] Concepts such as subculture and contraculture[20] and the recent enunciation of the structure of subterranean values among juvenile delinquents[21] call attention to the type of society which, we believe, is closer to social reality.

If subcultures refer to normative differences around which discrete groups are organized and if contraculture refers to those values which find their most prominent expression in conflict with the larger culture, the subterranean values are those which lie in the shadowy area between these two—"values, that is to say, which are in conflict or in competition with other deeply held values but which are still recognized and accepted by many."[22] The structure of subterranean values is such that they are not held merely by one of a number of opposed groups, but rather are widely held among different groups with varying attitudinal and situational orientations. Thus, positive orientations toward seeking thrills, employing "pull" or other forms of chicanery to "get ahead," and the use of violence are found throughout American society, but their expression among certain juveniles is labeled delinquent and regarded as deviant. The existence of a structure of pervasive but subterranean values suffused by divergences in orientation and attitude provides for the ubiquitous ambiguity in society.

Typically this ambiguity finds its expression in the quarrel over means and ends. Some commentators of the campus revolts will say that they agree with the goals of the students but cannot approve of the violent means they employ to attain them. However, they will—albeit grudgingly at times—approve of police and national guard use of those same means to suppress student demonstrations. Violence is one of the subterranean values of American culture. Officially condemned when practiced for private gain, vengeance, or thrills, violence is sometimes condoned when carried out in "just" retaliation, and usually praised and encouraged when justified by national policy.

Violence, then, is part of the American way of life.[23] It stands, so to speak, in the wings during all dramas of confrontation, struggles over values, and debates over rights—waiting to be called upon by any side when other more peaceable measures fail. Even the strategy of non-violence, employed for a brief time in the Civil Rights Movement by Martin Luther King, Jr., the Congress of Racial Equality, and the Student Non-Violent Coordinating Committee, was ultimately predicated in a dialectical sense upon the deep roots of violence in American mores. Non-violence foundered because it could not overcome—and indeed did not try to attack directly—the personal and social significance of violence for demonstrating manhood and dignity and its political efficacy in long-term struggles.[24]

Ambivalence about violence, which today finds expression in debate over the campus revolts, is endemic in the history of American social struggles. Before the Civil War, Abolitionists divided over pacifistic and pragmatic modes of liberating Negro slaves.[25] During the struggle to legitimize the collective bargaining rights of workers, violence was employed on all sides together with much rhetoric denouncing the use of force to settle social issues.[26] Indeed, the model of collective bargaining established by the labor movement, and embodied also in international diplomacy,[27] is today used as part of the rhetoric by which violence is denounced.

One reason why collective bargaining is not the initial step in campus struggles is that it presupposes that each side has something the other wishes, some kind of a bargaining position. Students, however, have no bargaining position qua students, since there is nothing except their presence in sufficient numbers in classrooms to justify teaching which the faculty or administration wants. In the absence of anything to bargain with, they are petitioners whose requests and recommendations may be politely ignored, promptly pigeonholed, or peremptorily dismissed. In order to convert their status from petitioners to bargainers, students picket an administrator, occupy a building, or shut down a campus. The more polite forms of bargaining that are recognized as reasonable by most members of society are for the most part foreclosed to students until they have engaged in acts of force or violence that are anathema to a great many.[28]

For some sectors of the community, however, the ideology of rebellion strikes a sound note of approval. Revolting students espouse equality in their attack on racism; democracy in their assertion of the right to do one's own thing; due process in their demand for proper treatment by police and judges; and peace in their desertion and deprecation of American wars. All of these values are also espoused in various ways and with varying degrees of qualification by large segments of the dominant society.[29] However, despite the students' "Americanism," these value components are likely to go unperceived or to be woefully distorted by those elements of the population who are not in harmony with the American social scene because they are suffering the pangs of a particular kind of anomie—the upwardly or downwardly mobile, the newly retired, the new urbanites, and so on—but are not revolutionary. The displaced Iowa farmer, for example, living in penurious retirement in southern California, is likely to see the student revolt, not in terms of its Americanist values, but rather as a form of exotic, incomprehensible, and decidely un-American activity. And in their commentaries, political leaders, aware of the context of ambiguity in which students couch their claims, are likely to seek to separate the American value components of which they approve from the particular activities which they despise.

The stable middle class in America—denigrated by the term WASP in both academic and revolutionary circles—is also likely to suffer from twinges of anxiety over its inability either to fully identify or entirely reject the current youth revolt. As Parsons has shown,[30] there is in America an identification with youth and youthful values that prevents a wholesale rejection of their style of life. Thus it is possible to regard young people as wrong, inept, and impatient, but at the same time to admire their outspoken candor, refreshing wit, and youthful exuberance.[31] Their over-zealousness may be condemned when it is employed for the wrong purposes, but at the same time their honesty and courage may be admired as appropriate, or indulged because of the assumption that it will be so short-lived.

A special group likely to feel ambivalence about the student revolt is the faculty. During the 1950s faculty complained bitterly about their students and labeled them a "silent generation." What was needed, said the faculty, was a politically aware and socially conscious student body. Now there can be no complaint that the students are both politically aware and socially conscious, and many faculty find themselves looking back upon the pastoral campus life of the fifties with guilty nostalgia. Moreover, intellectuals occupy a frustrating position in the social structure, training students who will assume positions in the corporate establishment that are more richly rewarded than their own.[32] The current revolt against the Establishment is silently applauded because it attacks elements of the society toward which the faculty is antipathetic, but at the same time is feared because of its general anti-intellectualism and its particular interest in controlling hiring, retention, and tenure of faculty. Faculty find themselves torn between their admiration for and fears of the students in revolt.

In sum, there is sufficient ambivalence within the larger culture toward student ideology to facilitate its continuance in spite of powerful forces of opposition. Americans in general, and faculty in particular, may be partly convinced that there is "something to what the kids are saying." This ambivalence tends toward limiting the disbelief and rejection held by non-students. Moreover, the ambivalence acts as a support of the students insofar as they can interpret the partial agreement of the larger society with their own beliefs as a half-way house to full-scale adoption or as the hesitating steps in the right direction of those who are on the road to enlightenment.

The effectiveness of the five mechanisms outlined above in maintaining the ideology is to be understood in large measure in terms of account-structuring, a phenomenon to which we now turn.

Accounts

Ideology serves as a legitimation for courses of action. In a general sense, a revolutionary ideology provides a definition of the current situation, a hazy but promising view of a better future, and a catalogue of grievances against the present social order that argue for its abandonment or overthrow. On the level of interaction such legitimations take the form of accounts.[33] An account is a linguistic device employed whenever an action is subjected to valuative inquiry. Accounts appear as statements made by social actors to relieve themselves of culpability for untoward or unanticipated acts.

In general, there are two types of accounts—excuses and justifications. An excuse is an admission that the act in question is bad, wrong, or inept, coupled with a denial of full responsibility. A justification is an admission of full responsibility for the act in question coupled with a denial that it was wrongful. In the case of the ideology of student revolt, justifications are the more prominent form of account since they assert the positive qualities of an act in the face of the general society's claim to the contrary.

Justifications may utilize a *universal* counterstatement to the original accusation, claiming that, in contrast to the accuser's position, the act in question is everywhere recognized as acceptable; or a *particularistic* one in which the act in question is recognized as generally impermissible, but situationally appropriate. Four of the well-known "techniques of neutralization" employed by Sykes and Matza[34] to explain how juveniles commit crimes without feeling like criminals—the "denial of injury," "denial of victim," "condemnation of the condemners," and "appeal to loyalties"—are generalized justification types that have wider usage than the arena of juvenile delinquency and are of particular importance in the analysis of student rhetoric. In addition, the "sad tale"—a selective arrangement of facts or a reconstruction of biography —and an appeal to the positive aspects of "self-fulfillment" are employed as justificatory accounts.

Denial
of Injury

Employing this account, a person acknowledges that he did commit a particular act, but he asserts that it was permissible to do so since no injury was sustained. Students who occupy a campus building point out that they injured no one, destroyed no *important* property, and committed no *serious* transgressions. (In some cases the students have pointed out that they cleaned the building before leaving it.) The same type of account is given with respect to rifling the desks of campus administrators. No injury was committed since the students only lifted the administrative veil from papers that should have been made public in the ordinary course of events. As Mark Rudd, leader of the Columbia uprising, said in distinguishing between what would have been a truly injurious act as opposed to what the students actually did, "If Grayson Kirk had had a mistress and we had found his letters to her while we spent time in his office, we certainly wouldn't have released them."[35] When students take over an empty lot owned by a university, plant grass, erect swings and slides, and invite the public to enjoy it, they regard the university's forcible closure of the recreational area as unjust since no injury was done to anyone by their establishment of a "people's park."

Denial
of Victim

Employing this account, a person asserts the position that the questioned action was permissible since the victim deserved the injury. Consider that part of the student ideology transforms persons and statuses from their positions of dignity and respect into characters and roles deserving of obloquy and scorn. Policemen who employ clubs and tear gas in upholding the social order become "pigs"; university administrators who limit the number of Negroes eligible for admission to the college are "honky liberals"; and scientists who do research on atomic, biological, and chemical warfare contribute to the "aggressive imperialism" of United States foreign policy. Just as juveniles justify their attacks on certain men because they are "queer" and deserve to be beaten up, so students in revolt may justify their injuries to policemen, professors, and physicists on the grounds that these dangerous and evil types are deserving of neither protection nor compassion.

Condemnation
of the Condemners

Employing this account, a person admits performing an untoward act but asserts its irrelevancy because others who are part of or protected by the society that condemns him commit similar or worse acts and are neither apprehended, castigated nor punished, and in some cases are praised. Students who are criticized for occupying a building, establishing a people's park, or using drugs may point out that United States military forces are doing far more damage in "occupying" Vietnam, that urban "renewal" destroys people's homes and uproots valuable natural and cultural settings, and that the Establishment's support of the tobacco and alcohol industries does at least as much harm as their own use of marijuana. In the dialogue over culpability, the student shifts the conversation away from the allegedly reprehensible nature of his own act onto the perhaps unnoticed and certainly unpunished activities of those who condemn him.

Appeal
to Higher Loyalties

In this account, a person justifies his behavior on the grounds that it served the interests of another person, of a group, or of a dream to which he owes unbreakable allegiance. Students have been arrested, unjustly in their own eyes, when they came to the aid of a fellow-student being beaten by a policeman. The campus communities, hippie neighborhoods, racial ghettos, and revolutionary circles build up a significant sense of loyalty among their members—loyalty which may find its expression in a sense of joint commitment that transcends public law, social mores, and personal morality. Finally, those students who are committed to the "revolution" owe a loyalty to it that by definition goes beyond the canons of law or standards of conduct associated with the prevailing society. For the true believer, all acts are justifiable if they can be interpreted as fulfilling the inevitable social change dictated by the wheel of history.

Sad Tales

When the sad tale is employed, the individual explains his behavior by reference to selected details of his immediate or biographical past. A sad tale is an excuse if the individual claims that the present situation in which he is involved is a product of a past over which he has had no control; it is a justification if the argument is that past events make the allegedly wrong behavior the logical or reasonable outcome of a correct line of action. Among the sad tales are those offered by persons, originally neutral, who found themselves caught up in the more hectic aspects of a demonstration and on the basis of their evaluation of those events determined to join the rebelling students. Still others are biographical reconstructions that conceive of participation in the student revolt as the natural and inevitable outcome of past life experiences. Thus students who are the children of erstwhile radical parents may conceive of their present involvement in the campus revolt as the inexorable effect of their upbringing in the revolutionary tradition; while students whose parents are conservative may be living out a generational backlash that finds expression and justification in the revolt against current society.

Self-fulfillment

In this account, persons explain that their behavior is righteous and unworthy of condemnation because of the sense of euphoric completeness which it evokes. Such justifications are quite common among users of marijuana and hallucinogenic drugs. Thus, in a world supposedly built on hypocrisy, sham, and mediated experiences, "tripping out" is justified on the grounds that it "turns-on a participant and bathes him in the raw sensuous-emotional experiencing of the living world which lies behind our concocted world-screens."[36] Self-fulfillment is also found in student justifications of the "communes" established in occupied buildings. What made these associations valuable for themselves was the deep and abiding sense of community which they created. Living together for days at a time on meager rations, makeshift amenities, and under pressures that might produce major panic, the commune dwellers developed a sense of solidarity that fulfilled at the same time that it transcended self. As one student striker remarked, "The communes are a better high than grass."[37]

Ideology does not exist in a vacuum. It is reforged and modified in the day-to-day experiences of the students. The "deviancies" which are justified by the ideology not only include those elements of the official culture which are specifically rejected but also those activities which are begun under conditions of stress and urgency during the course of the revolt. Accounts are a "cumulative" building up of a set of excuses and justifications for innovative or forbidden activities undertaken in the course of revolutionary events. When students at Columbia University occupied a building to protest administration heartlessness in constructing a gymnasium on land housing impoverished Negroes, they found themselves facing a practical problem. There was only one toilet, but the protesters numbered both men and women in their group. The ideology of liberation provided an account for the proffered solution:

> The influx of female radicals caused a problem on the third floor of Ferres Booth, where there is no ladies' room. The men's room was immediately designated as "liberated" and was used for the rest of the occupation by both sexes simultaneously.[38]

Ideology also provided accounts for further acts that would help realize the revolutionary aims. During the Columbia strike the presence of women in buildings held under police siege for days raised the question of whether standard female duties such as cooking and washing would be continued. A poster provided grounds for women to realize liberation from the drudgery associated with domesticity:

> To all Women:
> You are in a liberated area. You are urged to reject the traditional role of housekeeper unless, of course, you feel this is the role that allows for creative expression. Speak up! Use your brains![39]

Finally, the current ideology provides a general account by which members can justify their refusal to go along with their compatriots' particular brand of revolutionary or liberating acts. "I'm doing my own thing" is often sufficient ground for non-compliance since "doing one's thing," the quintessence of individualism and personalism, is one of the cardinal tenets of student ideology. Just as the statement "I'm having family problems" will justify a person's mood of listlessness, refusal to work, angry response to trifles, and tearful breakdowns, so the statement "I'm doing my thing, man!" will justify refusal to smoke marijuana, non-involvement in a strike, withdrawal from a commune, and adoption of middle-class dress. Clearly, then, this single account will stand for and justify a wide variety of events, and the efficacy of this account depends precisely on the shared "background expectancies" (i.e., unstated assumptions) of others with whom the speaker interacts. "Doing one's thing" strikes a resonant and familiar note among student activists, and thus provides ground for remaining an individual in the face of pressures of group conformity.

Often it is personally convenient or socially tactical not to offer an account for deviant behavior. This is especially the case if one believes that his account will not be honored, will be the source of further embarrassing or annoying inquiries, or will be the case for injury or punishment. Thus there are strategies to avoid giving accounts. The following are prominent.

Mystification

When the strategy of mystification is employed, a person admits he is not meeting the standards of conduct approved by his accuser, but follows this by pointing out that, although there are adequate and sound reasons for his seemingly untoward behavior, the accuser cannot be told what they are. For racial minorities, the current ideology of nationalism provides a fine opportunity to mystify whites. To all questions about conduct, a black militant might reply, "You wouldn't understand, you're white."

Mystification can also be created by the employment of props and idiom, style and demeanor which puts the questioner in the unenviable position of hearing an answer but not knowing its meaning. The manner employed by the black students occupying Hamilton Hall to respond to sociologist Immanuel Wallerstein's questions provides a good example:

> At 2 p.m. the two professors climbed over the file cabinets and chairs that formed the Hamilton barricades and were ushered into Dean Platt's office, which the steering committee had established as its headquarters. According to Sam Coleman, Cicero Wilson sat behind the main desk, clearly in charge. Wilson would look at Wallerstein who would ask a question, and then look at one of his colleagues who would answer. When the student—Bill Sales or Ray Brown—finished, Wilson's eyes

would return to Wallerstein who would then pose another
question. . . . The professors tried to discover exactly what the
blacks' position was, but ran up against a wall of reserve and
formality.[40]

As Wallerstein described it, "The point of this tactic was, I think,
that wrapped in mystery, they felt they could get more concessions."[41]

Referral

Using the strategy of referral, the individual says, in effect, "I know
I'm not meeting your expectations, but if you wish to know why,
please see . . . ." Typically, referral is a ploy open to the subordinate
members of a movement who can insist that all queries about conduct
and goals be addressed to their superiors. Subordinates and leaders may
also avoid accounts by sending the interrogator to the experts. Black
militants may refer inquiries to Eldridge Cleaver's *Soul on Ice*,[42]
members of the Students for a Democratic Society to the *Port Huron
Statement*, and marijuana users to the *Book of Grass*.[43] Mystification
and referral can be combined by referring the inquiry to persons so
exotic or readings so arcane that the interrogator will be left in a state
of perplexity and confusion. Thus students who claim that their strange
behavior derives from the philosophy of Gurdjieff[44] or who practice
rites in accordance with the *Teachings of Don Juan*[45] are likely to put
off giving a full and complete account and to discourage the ordinary
interrogator from further questions as well.

Identity Switching

In this maneuver, a person indicates to his accuser or interrogator that
he is not playing the role that the latter assumes. The multiple identities possessed by young people provide a repertoire of roles which may
be donned or doffed as tactics demand. Young people are, *inter alia*,
students, rebels, victims of the draft, members of the exploited populace, and possessors of racial, religious, and national heritages. When
called to account as a student, a young man can reply, "I'm not a
student; I'm a man." When addressed as a Negro, a person of African
descent can retort, "I'm not a Negro; I'm a black man." When reminded of his obligation as a citizen, a zealous youth can respond, "I'm
not a citizen since I cannot control my destiny; I'm a revolutionary."

Identity switching may be phased, employing each new role for its
interactional payoffs and then discarding it when its usefulness is at an
end. Youths who occupy a campus building might appeal for public
sympathy on the grounds that they are merely students seeking a re-

dress of grievances. Later they may couch their demands in terms of minority status. And, finally, they may justify their own behavior to one another in terms of their membership in a revolutionary vanguard. As this discussion suggests, identities are not the only thing that may be switched, but audiences as well, so that an appropriate identity may be adopted before different audiences. There are risks in this, since one is liable to exposure from persons in one audience who have seen the same persons in a different performance before another audience. However, audience segregation and a rhetoric of accounts to justify the assumption of different identities might suffice as protection.

In sum, accounts provide a linguistic device whereby untoward actions may be excused or justified. These accounts ultimately depend on shared expectations of those who give and receive them. Ideology provides the framework for rhetorics of justification, the large society's ambivalence provides a shroud of common understanding to those on both sides of the struggle, and strategies of account avoidance partially protect "deviants" against embarrassing mistakes or tactical errors.

Fun
in Games

To further clarify the structure of motivations sustaining student revolt, we shall now turn to an analysis in terms of a game-theoretic framework, in its simple social-psychological form. Our formulation of the game approach employs dimensions of social-psychology opened up in symbolic-interactionist thought and developed by Erving Goffman.[46] We shall be seriously concerned with the fact that the student revolt has many of the qualities of a game including its most basic and commonsense one: games are *fun*. Fun experiences have their own consequences, not the least of which is the desire to continue them. Briefly summarized, our point here is that the ideology of revolution and the actions taken in its name create a game-like situation which in turn generates psychological satisfactions that may best be termed "fun." And this fun, in turn, serves as an added motivation to continue beliefs in the ideology and to take actions in its name. Thus, the continuity of the student revolt, its persistent and repetitious character, may be understood in light of the fact that there is fun in games.

Fun—that amorphous sensation of exhilaration—arises in part simply because people are engaged in daring or deceptive attacks on social order. But how, specifically, does a particular violation of the law, customs, or codes of conduct become a pleasurable event? The particular violative act does not, as such, automatically generate a pleasant feeling. Nor does any act. Rather, acts must be defined as pleasurable[47] by significant others associated with the act in question. How individuals come to define smoking marijuana as a pleasurable act illustrates the role of significant others, and the operation of what Goffman has called "transformation rules"[48] in inducing a favorable reaction to an innovative and potentially tense experience. Apparently new users of marijuana may not experience a "high" from their first "joint," may not perceive the effects of the drug or relate felt effects to drug use, and may not enjoy the sensations which they do experience. Hence it often happens that a friend who is an experienced user serves as a guide explaining to the novice just exactly how to inhale in order to activate the drug, what to recognize—excessive hunger, rubbery legs, etc.—as signs of a high, and how to treat the ambiguous sensations— dizziness, the sense of going insane, nausea—as pleasurable. Without this guidance and assistance in converting a new and sometimes panic-producing experience into a euphoric episode, the individual might sense that nothing at all had happened or he might become so frightened by what he feels that he never tries the drug again. In the course of the "learning" process, however, the novice usually develops a positive disposition toward marijuana, and later he exhibits his membership in the subculture of marijuana users when he answers "yes" to the question, "Is smoking grass fun?"

In the case of the student revolt, fun has to be learned also. Ideology itself assists in the educational process for much of the ideology insists precisely on this fact: revolution is fun. Figures close to the revolution have emphasized its fun elements. Abbie Hoffman writes of *Revolution for the Hell of It*,[49] urges Marxists to "have a good time,"[50] believes "in the politics of ecstasy,"[51] and next to "making love," he confesses to liking "to experience pleasure, to have fun."

> I enjoy blowing people's minds. You know, walking up to somebody and saying, "Would you hold this dollar for me while I go in that store and steal something?" The crazier the better. I like being crazy. Letting go. Losing control. Just doing what pops into my mind. I trust my impulses. I find the less I try to think through a situation, the better it comes off.[52]

He adds:

> I think fun and leisure are great. I don't like the concept of a movement built on sacrifice, dedication, respectability, anger, frustration and guilt. All those damn things. . . . When I say fun, I mean an experience so intense that you actualize your full

potential. You become LIFE. LIFE IS FUN. Political irrelevance is more effective than political relevance.[53]

Hoffman's book is a primer for would-be revolutionaries on the definition of fun. Fun becomes, as the multitude of examples in the book clearly indicates, the violation of "background expectancies," the sabotage of the "recipes-for-living" that every socialized member of a society knows. Social life everywhere is built upon a complex of invisible but important threads of meaning and predictability, which in ordinary situations exist only at the subliminal level of cognition.[54] The significance of these threads becomes manifest when a sudden interruption, a nasty surprise, or a remarkable violation of ordinary conceptions of inter-human trust occur. The ensuing breakdown of social relations raises to the cognitive foreground just those conditions, heretofore non-conscious, which are the *sine qua non* of social existence. Thus, in a remarkably revealing experiment, Harold Garfinkel instructed students to behave like boarders in their own homes.[55] At first parents were annoyed, amused, or concerned for their children's health. However, when the parents had exhausted all "rational" explanations for their children's behavior, they became mystified, anxious, and, in some cases, incensed. Behavior that is presented must be accounted for according to the rules governing both normal behavior and "normal" departures from it. When people behave abnormally and no reason for it can be adduced, the basic threads of society are subverted, a true revolution is underway.

Violating the conditions of trust that underlie the normative order is not immediately understood as enjoyable. These violations have to be made into fun in order to be perceived as such. Hoffman does just that for his followers in numerous accounts of activities which he defines as fun. He explains why one day, after a group of Negroes had been arrested on a pot bust, he lay down in front of a police station, kicked in the glass case containing police trophies, and used obscenities on the officers who had until then been ignoring him:

> People ask me why I did what I did at the station house and I told them a story similar to the one I just told here, but it was all bullshit. I really did it because it was fun.[56]

At another point in his book Hoffman explains how open-faced robbery of a university cafeteria is fun:

> Last fall I spoke at Cornell and announced "The food here is free!" and twenty of us walked into the cafeteria, loaded our

trays with hamburgers, Cokes, and pies and walked out without paying. We sat in the dining hall laughing and slapping each other on the back. . . .[57]

Destroying a classroom and disrupting the instructional program also becomes enjoyable:

> We appeared at Brooklyn College and announced "The class-room environment is free," unscrewed desk tops and transformed them into guns, passed out incense and art, wrote Black Board on the door, switched off the lights and continued in darkness, announcing that the security guard was one of us, freeing him through the destruction of his identity, and in general doing whatever spontaneously came to mind.[58]

In Hoffman's literary images, the movement in the universities becomes a great revolution conducted as if it were a carnival. The disruption of classes, the sabotage of bells to announce the end of classes ("Bring alarm clocks to school and have them ring on the half hour instead of the hour"),[59] and the breakdown of the academic order are the pre-conditions for having one big ball: "You can buy a small Japanese tape recorder and a few speakers from a junkyard for about twenty-five dollars. Some careful camouflaging and you can suddenly turn the school into a huge discotheque."[60]

Revolutionaries have also to be taught to enjoy the effects of their actions. After a classroom has been destroyed, a building occupied, a strike attacked by the police, feelings including anxiety, panic, shame, and guilt are likely among the perpetrators. The group spirit that grew up in committing the very acts whose consequences they now must hear is helpful. In addition, ordinary activities—providing food, creating amenities, treating the sick—take up time, require cooperative spirit, and evoke hidden talents. The very pace of activity in the first hours of a building take-over often prevents the pause for reflection that might produce shame or second thoughts. But in a long siege, as was the case in the Columbia strike, the potentiality of a pall falling over the group is great. In Columbia's "liberated" halls, balloons and streamers festooned the occupied areas, decisions were made by employing participatory democracy, voluntary committees sprang up to carry out innovative activities, a wedding ceremony was performed, and a pianist played Chopin. In Hamilton Hall, occupied by black students, a girl reported:

> The spirit inside was beautiful; there was singing, talking, dancing to music from small phonographs, watching TV, participat-

ing in the interminable meetings. One student, after spending five days in the building, could not sleep in his bed at home; he had to curl up on the floor.[61]

The cumulative effect of living on sandwiches and oranges, sleeping in "liberated areas," attending endless meetings to decide democratically on nearly every aspect of living, and just spending time in a cramped but communal environment may produce the euphoric and eudaemonic effect of a "beautiful experience," an "honest" existence, a "joyful" time—in short, of fun.

Strategic Game Components

Let us again consider the properties of games and their application to campus revolts. In most games there is a game-defined *opponent*, minimal game *resources*, and a clear notion of *goals*. It is also true of campus revolts that there must be a defined enemy, available facilities for action, and some aims in mind, the attainment of which will be defined as victory.

Opponents

The student protesters have many identifiable opponents. College and university presidents, deans, admission officers, financial aid officers, certain professors and researchers on government projects, and the police are among the most notable and readily available enemies. However, the designation of these statuses as hostile did not arise at the beginning of this era of protest. Indeed, the turn to the campus as a site for student revolts is a recent development of a movement that was once centered on the military, industrial, and political rather than educational institutions. Eldridge Cleaver has perceptively suggested that the evolution of white youthful revolt against modern America has gone through four stages ending with the revolt on campus:

> First there was an initial recoiling away, a rejection of the conformity which America expected, and had always received, soon or later, from its youth. . . . Because of the publicity and self-advertisements of the more vocal rebels, this period has

come to be known as the beatnik era, although not all of the youth affected by these changes thought of themselves as beatniks. . . .

The second stage arrived when these young people, having decided emphatically, that the world, and particularly the U.S.A., was unacceptable to them in its present form, began an active search for roles they could play in changing the society. . . . The non-beat disenchanted white youth were attracted magnetically to the Negro revolution, which had begun to take on a mass, insurrectionary tone. . . .

The third stage, which is rapidly drawing to a close, emerged when white youth started joining Negro demonstrations in large numbers. . . . In fact they had begun to transform it into something broader, with the potential of encompassing the whole of America in a radical reordering of society.

The fourth stage, now in its infancy, sees these white youth taking the initiative, using techniques learned in the Negro struggle to attack problems in the general society. The classic example of this new energy in action was the student battle on the UC campus at Berkeley, California—the Free Speech Movement.[62]

Students and other dissidents had in the early years of the modern protest movement discussed and planned various kinds of non-violent and militant activities on college campuses but carried them out outside the university grounds. For the most part these activities were only partially successful, and some were dismal failures. The early civil rights sit-ins, freedom rides, and marches in the South succeeded in forcing federal legislation but did not solve the social and economic inequalities that marred Negro life. Moreover, early successes raised hopes for a more promising reordering of society that not only did not materialize, but seemed to recede further with every advance. Finally, in opposition to their much vaunted integration into a white-dominated society, young Negro leaders redefined their goals in terms of black autonomy and a pluralistic conception of society. If the civil rights movement only partially resolved some issues and raised other more difficult ones, the anti-war movement turned out to be nearly a total failure. Attacks on selective service offices, the public burning of draft cards, and the attempts to halt troop trains came to naught. The war in Vietnam continued, the presidential candidacies of youth sympathizers such as McCarthy and Kennedy were destroyed by political machines and assassination, the murders of Medgar Evers, Malcolm X, and Martin Luther King, Jr., testified to the deep-seated racism in the American body politic, and the total societal reconstruction that loomed so large in dissenters' thoughts seemed further away than ever.

The protest movement then engaged in a dramatic shift in its emphases on priorities and of its locus of operation. It was the campus that had to be "radicalized" first in order to change society. Rather than the older perception of the university as a haven for study, a refuge for critical discussion, and a source for intellectual and moral inspiration, youthful radicals have come to see it as the symbol of the recalcitrance by which organized society impedes progress and the source of substantive support for racism, war, and poverty. Even though the "war" is against racial oppression, grinding poverty, avaricious imperialism, and socio-cultural destruction in America, the battles were to be held on the college campuses. The enemies might be the racist Southern senators, the profit-hungry corporate capitalists, and the white power structure, but the opponents were closer at hand—the officials of the campus. A speech by Bill Sales, an active member of the Students' Afro-American Society at Columbia University during the protest of the building of a gymnasium illustrates this symbolic redefinition:

> If you're talking about revolution, if you're talking about identi-
> fying with the Vietnamese struggle, if you're talking about
> supporting German students, you don't need to go to Rocke-
> feller Center, dig? You don't need to go marching downtown.
> There's one oppressor—in the White House, in Low Library, in
> Albany, New York. You strike a blow at the gym, you strike a
> blow for the Vietnamese people. . . . You strike a blow at the
> gym and you strike a blow against the assassin of Dr. Martin
> Luther King, Jr. You strike a blow at Low Library and you
> strike a blow for the freedom fighters in Angola, Mozambique,
> Portuguese Guinea, Zimbabwe, South Africa.[63]

Campus courses and the curriculum are now regarded by student radicals as at best irrelevant to the real needs and social aspirations of today's youth. But at the same time, college policies, specialized research, and the complex interrelationships between the university and the government are quite relevant to the improvement of military imperialism, political control, economic exploitation, social oppression, and personal misery. The opponents of the student radicals are all around the campus. They include military recruitment teams and ROTC programs; job interviewers from Dow Chemical Corporation,

makers of napalm; professors working on secret government projects
such as the infamous "Project Camelot"; CIA and FBI agents posing
as students; deans and financial aids officers who control student activities and scholarship funds; and all those spokesmen for the establishment appointed to university posts by a cooperative administration.
By turning away, temporarily, from the institutions and officers of the
larger society and concentrating their efforts on the local college
campus, student radicals reduced the enemy to manageable size without
de-escalating the ultimate scope of their movement.

Resources

The redefinition of the campus and its environs as the arena for student
revolt raised issues of the available resources which this kind of entity
provided and required. The spatial and temporal characteristics of
the campus itself were converted into resources, as we shall now
examine.

A college campus is usually an enclosed area, bounded on all sides
by a city or town, or isolated in the countryside. Precisely because of
its bounded identity, the campus gave the elements of revolt a distinct
reality and a definite locus for operation. Just as a chess game must be
played on a board, a tennis game on a court, and a football game on a
playing field, so the "game" of campus revolt must be played on
a well-marked territory. Consider by contrast an alternative situation.
Suppose all higher education was conducted at home by television
broadcasts from a distant center. Suppose tests were taken individually,
and the entire administration of grades, enrollment, registration, and
matriculation were handled by mail. Suppose further that professors
were flown in from all parts of the country for their regular broadcasts,
research was carried on in secret, and that the military and industry
recruited their personnel by announcements over the air, as in the case
of commercial advertisements for cigarettes and soap. In other words,
suppose that going to college could be undertaken without any spatial
definition of "a college" coming into play. Campus revolts, as such,
could not occur.

The campus is an available resource for generating a particular kind
of event, though one that was not foreseen by its designers, and realizing certain kinds of identities, unattainable without it. The fact that a
single building houses a computer center in which all student records
are processed and stored makes that building an ideal object for attack
in a movement which denigrates society's refusal to treat its inhabitants

as humans. The fact that a dean may spend long hours in his office, reading reports, writing memos, and worrying over campus affairs makes the "capture" and "imprisonment" of a dean by an army of five or six hundred students—what in Bengal is called the Gherao[64]—a realizable possibility. The campus revolt, like a game of chess or baseball, is a world-building event. It is only in such a revolt that one can "liberate the library," "take over the administration building," or "co-opt the study body leaders," just as it is only in baseball that one can "ground out to third," and only in chess that one can "castle."

Time, as well as space, takes on a new and strategic meaning in the student revolt. Campus life has a certain rhythm which, in turn, tends to be incorporated into the revolt and employed as a tactic as well by all sides. Any aficionado of the Berkeley scene will confirm that the daylight hours from 11 a.m. to 3 p.m. are the time for maximum campus disruption, that noon in front of Sproul Hall is usually *when* as well as *where* the action is, and that seminars held from 7 to 9 p.m. are not likely to be interrupted by strikers. Moreover, the division of the day into hours of class and hours in which one is free to do as one pleases; of the week into five school days, separated by a weekend during which teaching is suspended; of the year into quarters or semesters with spring, Christmas, and voluntary summer vacations—all these divisions are time tracks which count in the campus revolt as well as in the regular campus life.

One way of understanding the temporal qualities of campus revolt is to perceive the latter in terms of "time-in" and "time-out."[65] "Time-in" refers to the time period in which a discrete sequence of activity is played out; "time-out" refers to a respite in any activity sequence during which rules and roles related to that activity may be relaxed or revoked. Of course time-out on one activity often signals time-in on another. In the case of campus revolts sequestered space and the periodicity of normal activities make possible the switch from permissible to prohibited acts with little difficulty. Professors at San Francisco State College occasionally reported on the bizarre phenomenon of lecturing to a dutiful class on a dry and dull subject, while their own eyes could not resist shifting to the scene of violent action being played out on the grass outside the window. Students could excuse themselves from a coffee date by glancing at their watch and saying, "See you later; I have to join a demonstration"; and young people frequently moved from classroom to confrontation in accordance with their campus schedule. Moreover, administrators and city officials can make plans with respect to decisions, strategy, and tactics on the basis of their knowledge of just when students will be on campus or away for vacations. Finally, the fact that the faculty and administrators are "permanent" figures on the campus while the students are there for only a four-year period permits the former to discount the demands of the latter as those of "birds-of-passage." ("You're only transitory birds," President Grayson Kirk once told a group of students who confronted him, "and therefore should not have a voice.")[66]

Time-out in one activity is usually looked at as a period in which people relax, engage in "unserious" activity, and pursue "unserious" affairs. However, precisely because it is looked at this way, time-out periods are useful in order to regroup forces, retrieve lost items, and recover strength. It may also be used for secret meetings, clandestine contacts, and treacherous moves. Thus, both college administrators and radical students might use Christmas vacations to plot new strategies, recruit new allies, and regain lost support. Popular but radical instructors may be given notice just before a summer semester is to begin so that they will not have time to drum up a student movement in their own behalf. And radical students might use the convenience of attending a classroom lecture in order to rest before entering a campus fray.

The problem created by time-out periods is the same as that created by another feature of the campus revolts—the deadline for demanded action; that is, both are subject to questions of credibility. In the case of any time-out on a revolt, opponents may be suspicious of just what the real meaning is of any cessation of confrontation. Similarly, when one side presents a set of demands and appends a notice that these must be met within a specific period, the other side must wonder whether the deadline is flexible or not. In both kinds of situation, information will be sought to confirm the credibility of the avowed definition of the situation. Since this information itself might be a tactical item in the revolt, the situation may take on the aspect of an information game in which one side—the seeker—tries to uncover independent evidence that the other side—the evader—tries to keep hidden or at least camouflaged.[67] Espionage, surveillance, and the use of "plants" and informers are not uncommon. An atmosphere of distrust and suspicion prevails, and each side is more than skeptical of the other's intentions and morality. The "paranoid" states thus produced will be a topic treated shortly.

Goals

In most games, there is both a conception of completion and of victory. In some games they coincide. A chess game, for example, is over when one player has placed the other's king in checkmate. But in other games termination and victory need not coincide. A football game is completed after one hour's playing time whether or not any side has scored. Termination and victory need not be concomitant features in a contest. In any game situation, understood rules govern just what constitutes the nature of victory, and whether termination and victory must coincide or not.

The campus revolt is similar to a complex game in this as well as other respects. Ideology defines victory and suggests—in rather vague terms—just what constitutes the termination of the revolt. But the ideology of the current revolt like that of many other revolts is not too clear on just what victory will look like, and, of course, places no exact time limit on termination. In practice, however, victory is perceived in terms of gradual increments of "liberation" obtained in every confrontation—greater freedom of speech, an ethnic studies program, resignation of an oppressive administrator—and in terms of the sense of psychological well-being and euphoria experienced by the participants. Thus, the FSM regarded the outcome of the conflict at Berkeley in 1964 as a victory in what might be termed one "round" of the general struggle; the black students at San Francisco State College may celebrate a victory if a Black Studies Curriculum is headed by a man of their choice; and many of the students who participate in the campus strikes, demonstrations, and revolts admit to experiencing a sense of life-change that is so exhilarating that any negative effects pale into insignificance beside it.

The coercive polarization of campus life into "left" and "right" factions is also seen as victory since it leads to accretions in the number of "radicalized" students. One goal is the removal of the liberal middle from campus affairs. At San Francisco State, the SDS leadership rejoiced at the downfall of two college presidents known for their democratic liberalism. These men are popular with the silent moderate-liberal majority. Any movement toward polarization and radicalization of the campus is seen as a victory.

Goals in the campus revolt, then, are both instrumental and expressive. Victories are perceived in terms of the partial social and libertarian gains obtained for various segments of society and sections of the university, in the addition of heretofore uncommitted elements to one of the polarized factions which constitute the radicals' idealized definition of a revolutionary situation, and—at least for the mass of participants in the revolt—in the eudaemonic and euphoric spirit which is liberated in the process of the revolt itself.

Revolt,
Paranoia
and Game
Theory

In concluding our discussion of the game properties of campus revolt, we should like to mention the peculiar qualities of consciousness associated with persons involved in these conflicts.

Any encounter between two or more individuals may be analyzed as a game if the following conditions prevail: at least one of the interactants is aware or capable of being made aware that, in realizing his aims in the encounter, he must take into account the others' expectations of him, the others' expectations of what he expects of them, and vice versa.

Now, a moment's reflection will surely reveal that the quality of consciousness associated with any situation having the properties of a "game" is different from that associated with ordinary life. The latter is carried out, as Alfred Schutz has so persuasively argued, according to "cook book" knowledge:

> Most of our daily activities from rising to going to bed are of this kind. They are performed by following recipes reduced to automatic habits or unquestioned platitudes. This kind of knowledge is concerned only with the regularity as such of events in the external world irrespective of its origin. Because of this regularity it can be reasonably expected that the sun will rise to-morrow morning. It is equally regular, and it can, therefore, with as good reason be anticipated too that the bus will bring me to my office if I choose the right one and pay my fare.[68]

Game-theoretic behavior, on the other hand, evokes an entirely different quality to conscious states. Whereas in the routines of everyday life "clear and distinct experiences are intermingled with vague conjectures; suppositions and prejudices cross well-proven evidences; motives, means and ends, as well as causes and effects, are strung together without clear understanding of their real connections,"[69] in a game the situation is experienced as puzzling, the events as irregular, and the outcomes of one's actions as both problematic and crucial. A person in a "game" is forced back on himself, coerced by the situations, so to speak, into a state of reflection. Persons involved in game situations find themselves in a state of hyperconsciousness in which, rather than behaving according to the cook book recipes for living that ordinarily govern behavior, they are led to look over the particular situation in terms of its remote possibilities, hidden motives, camouflaged meanings, and undisclosed dangers. Such a situation arises quite regularly, in a one-sided way, for those persons suffering from some social or physical stigma which forces them to continually regard their world as problematic. As a result of possessing a stigma, an individual, according to Goffman,

> may be led into placing brackets around a spate of casual social interaction so as to examine what is contained therein for general themes. He can become "situation conscious" while normals present are spontaneously involved *within* the situation, the situation itself constituting for these normals a background of unattended matters.[70]

In addition to those, like the stigmatized, who experience a constantly problematic world, the state of hyperconsciousness is also evoked by quite ordinary persons when their routine world temporarily breaks down. When an old friend suddenly behaves in a bizarre way, when regular practices are suddenly changed, when institutionalized arrangements are violated, those involved find themselves "outside" the everyday world, spectators and participants in a situation that is without immediate definition and predictable outcome. At such times persons experience not only a heightened awareness of what would otherwise be unattended elements of the environment, but also a sense of suspicion about the meanings of these elements. In other words, when normal people are in abnormal situations they are likely to experience and exhibit a state of mind which a clinical investigator might describe as "paranoid."[71]

Now campus revolts constitute a dramatic interruption of the ordinary routines of college life. Whereas the official definition of a college includes the idea that its inhabitants form a community, sharing a common outlook, and participating jointly and separately in the diverse activities that make up the learning, teaching, and discovering of knowledge, the revolt forces a jolting realization that the much-vaunted community does not exist. Moreover, the regular activities—going to class, taking examinations, visiting professors in their offices—can no longer be assumed to be proper or safe. The administration building— once only a place to visit in order to pay a library fine, complain to a dean, or file a thesis—now is both symbol and battleground for an idea that has been forcibly activated: "liberation." New faces and activities are now on the campus in great numbers and deadly variety:

police and troops, and the beating, gassing, and arresting of students, faculty, and by-standers, not a few of whom are innocent. And finally new roles, innovative styles, and suddenly inspired statuses appear. While chaos and disorganization may appear as the most exact description of the situation, in fact, there is a new, different, and, as far as those involved are concerned, not yet clear organization coming into existence.

In such a situation, students, faculty, and administrators often find that the most routine situations take on the character of unrehearsed drama. What would be quite ordinary and casual social situations are now perceived as fraught with danger or opportunity. A student at the University of California reported how he carefully mapped the safest route from his home to the administration building—via side streets, basements, and building to building sprints across campus—so that he could file his doctoral dissertation without encountering either student demonstrators or police.[72] The aura of suspicion that prevails can lead to strange encounters. Two professors, strolling up one of the lanes that border Telegraph Avenue in Berkeley were accosted by a coed who had been watching them carefully, accused of being plain clothes policemen, and cursed abusively for the pernicious surveillance they supposedly kept on students. At first they enjoyed the humor involved in their mistaken identity, but as the obscene invective increased in intensity and vitriol, they too became angry, produced identification, and attempted to shame or mollify their accuser. At Columbia, terror and romantic idealism were combined in the spectacle of the black and white student leaders debating ideology upstairs in a "liberated" building while down below blacks angrily asserted their differences with white demonstrators: "It was fascinating—here they were presenting this grandiose vision of revolution and a new world, while the blacks were downstairs scaring the shit out of everyone."[73]

An air of apprehension hangs over a scene that once was marked by routinized activity and ordinary affairs. In such a situation people find themselves pausing to consider their actions much more than before, and looking over the situation very carefully before proceeding. The orientation bears something of the character of an audience at a theatrical performance. As one student put it:

> The essential nature of politics is theater, and this became abundantly clear at the confrontations between the strikers and the police. Sproul Plaza becomes an outdoor theater, with picketers on stage, the police waiting in the wings, and a great mass of spectators, milling around, waiting. Everyone is at the

same time actor and spectator. It might seem that the people on
the line are the actors, but if you spend any time on the line
you realize that there is little to do but wait and watch.[74]

The activist on either side in such a situation becomes suspicious of
objects and persons in his environment that under ordinary circumstances would not occasion even a pause for reflection. A black student
from Africa, who had joined other black students in occupying Columbia's Hamilton Hall, was chastised by strike leaders for exchanging a
few words on an academic matter with faculty negotiator Professor
Immanuel Wallerstein.[75] A white professor was accused of insensitivity
to the race question when he offered to substitute himself in place of
a bleeding black student as an escort for a black woman professor trying to get to her car in the midst of the police-striker fight at San
Francisco State College.[76] Numerous other illustrations could be cited.

The participant in a campus revolt must explore, in game-theoretic
fashion, the possibilities of all encounters. Faculty, administrators, and
students—like good intelligence officers—become attuned to conceal-
ment and detection. The shift in orientation escalates from mild suspicion—"what is really going on?"—to a quasi-pathological conviction
that "something is going on behind my back." Students wonder just
what the "real" meaning is of any concessions made by faculty negotia-
tors; administrators worry about the "conspiratorial plot" that is being
hatched by the "small group" of "leaders," and whether these leaders
are in turn agents of a larger scheme of macrocosmic proportions. The
documents captured by students in the Columbia president's office
purportedly "proved" the truth of the university's pernicious involvement in the military-industrial oligarchy; the fact that Stokely Carmichael supported the black students in their Columbia revolt, Eldridge
Cleaver the FSM at Berkeley, and George Murray (a "minister" in the
Black Panthers) the San Francisco State strike "proves" that the revolts have a wider scope than campus reform. In other words, the
context of distrust encourages a mutual assessment of situations in
conspiratorial and paranoid ways—in the ways associated with "play"
in a serious "game."

To restate our argument: game play typically involves a reciprocation
of mutual assessments by all those engaged in play. When a game-like
situation occurs within an atmosphere of suspicion and distrust, these
assessments take the form of close inspection, mysterious intuitions,
anticipatory thinking, and the imputation to others of just those evil
motives that would require strategic planning. And these forms of
cognition in contexts other than that of the campus revolt are regarded

by clinicians as signs of pathology and especially paranoia. The pathological label can be rendered innocuous when we recognize the family resemblance between game situations and paranoia on the one hand and play and suspicion on the other.

The point has been made nicely by Lemert who, on the basis of careful research, has shown that the onset of paranoia is characterized by the discovery of a real conspiracy, which, in the absence of its recognition as such by others, comes to haunt the consciousness and disturb the emotional balance of the discoverer.[77] The behavior associated with the normal treatment of real conspiracies is not too different from that given in response to the supposed pseudo-community of conspirators that oppress the paranoid. In both situations there is heightened awareness, suspicion of motives, acute examination of seemingly trivial things, and the imputation of hostile intentions and remarkable cleverness to those under suspicion. On the campus during such a revolt neither students nor administrators saw themselves as "paranoid," though it was not uncommon for each to accuse the other of a paranoid behavior that poisoned the wells of what little community had survived.

Notes

[1]See J. L. Simmons, "On Maintaining Deviant Belief Systems," *Social Problems,* XI (Winter, 1964), 250-56.

[2]See Max Weber, *The Protestant Ethic and the Spirit of Capitalism* (New York: Charles Scribner, 1930), p. 178.

[3]Robert K. Merton, *Social Theory and Social Structure* (New York: The Free Press of Glencoe, 1968), pp. 476-77.

[4]See Kenneth Keniston, *Young Radicals* (New York: Harcourt, Brace, and World, 1968).

[5]See Richard R. Korn and Lloyd McCorkle, "The Reluctant Robbers," in *Deviance: The Interactionist Perspective,* eds. Earl Rubington and Martin S. Weinberg (New York: Macmillan, 1968), pp. 330-33.

[6]David Matza, *Delinquency and Drift* (New York: John Wiley, 1964), pp. 50-59.

[7]Quoted in Dorothy Rabinowitz, "Power in the Academy," *Commentary,* XLVII (June, 1969), 48.

[8]Noam Chomsky, *American Power and the New Mandarins* (New York: Pantheon Books, 1967), pp. 371-72.

[9]See Erving Goffman, "Where the Action Is," *Interaction Ritual* (Garden City: Doubleday Anchor, 1968), pp. 223-27.

[10]*Berkeley Barb,* VIII, No. 24 (June 13-19), 3.

[11]Tom Hayden, "Two, Three, Many Columbias," *Ramparts* (June 15, 1968), p. 40. Reprinted in *The Politics and Anti-Politics of the Young,* ed. Michael Brown (Beverly Hills, Calif.: Glencoe Press, 1969), p. 75.

[12]See Egon Bittner, "Radicalism and the Organization of Radical Movements," *American Sociological Review*, XXVIII (December, 1963), 928-40.

[13]Max Weber, *Economy and Society*, eds. Guenther Roth and Claus Wittich (New York: Bedminister Press, 1968), II, 450-51.

[14]See Reinhard Bendix and Seymour Martin Lipset, "Karl Marx' Theory of Social Classes," in *Class, Status, and Power*, eds. Reinhard Bendix and Seymour Martin Lipset (Glencoe: The Free Press, 1953), pp. 26-35.

[15]For the concept of home territory, see Stanford M. Lyman and Marvin B. Scott, "Territoriality: a Neglected Sociological Dimension," *Social Problems*, XV (Fall, 1967), 236-49.

[16]See Kenneth Keniston, "Heads and Seekers: Drugs on Campus, Counter-Cultures, and American Society," *The American Scholar*, XXXVIII (Winter, 1968-1969), 97-112.

[17]*Ibid.*, p. 107.

[18]*Loc. cit.*

[19]For a discussion of these concepts, see Stanford M. Lyman, "The Race Relations Cycle of Robert E. Park," *Pacific Sociological Review*, XI (Spring, 1968), 16-22.

[20]See J. Milton Yinger, "Contraculture and Subculture," *American Sociological Review*, XXV (October, 1960), 625-35.

[21]See David Matza and Gresham Sykes, "Juvenile Delinquency and Subterranean Values," *American Sociological Review*, XXVI (October, 1961), 712-19.

[22]*Ibid.*, p. 716.

[23]See *The History of Violence in America*, eds. Hugh Davis Graham and Ted Robert Gurr (New York: Bantam Books, 1969).

[24]See Inge Powell Bell, *CORE and the Strategy of Nonviolence* (New York: Random House, 1968), pp. 169-74.

[25]See Peter Brock, *Pacifism in the United States* (Princeton, N. J.: Princeton University Press, 1968), pp. 449-868.

[26]See Norman J. Ware, *The Labor Movement in the United States, 1860-1895* (New York: Vintage, 1929); and Joseph G. Rayback, *A History of American Labor* (New York: The Free Press, 1966).

[27]See Talcott Parsons, "Polarization of the World and International Order," *Berkeley Journal of Sociology*, VI (Spring, 1961), 115-34.

[28]See the insightful essay by Talcott Parsons, "Some Reflections on the Place of Force in Social Process," in *Internal War*, ed. Harry Eckstein (London: Collier-Macmillan, 1964), pp. 33-70.

[29]Thus San Francisco columnist Herb Caen writes: "It's not the long hair, the wild (and wonderful) clothes, their preference for marijuana over martinis, their renunciation of the materialistic goals that have brought plenty for some and peace for none. What really gnaws at the elders is the lurking fear, deep down inside, that the young people MAY BE RIGHT. Society can never forgive that." San Francisco *Chronicle*, "Sunday Punch" (July 7, 1969), p. 1.

[30]Talcott Parsons, "Age and Sex in the Social Structure of the United States," in *Essays in Sociological Theory* (New York: The Free Press of Glencoe, 1964), pp. 89-103.

[31]See, for example, James A. Michener, *America vs. America: The Revolution in Middle-Class Values* (New York: Signet, 1969).

[32]For a discussion of this theme, see Seymour Martin Lipset, *Political Man* (Garden City: Doubleday and Co., 1960), pp. 310-43.

[33]For an extended discussion of this point, see Marvin B. Scott and Stanford M. Lyman, "Accounts," *American Sociological Review,* XXXIII (February, 1968), 46-62.

[34]Gresham M. Sykes and David Matza, "Techniques of Neutralization," *American Sociological Review,* XXII (December, 1957), 664-70.

[35]Mark Rudd, "Symbols of the Revolution," in *Up Against the Ivy Wall,* ed. Jerry L. Alvorn (New York: Atheneum, 1968), p. 297.

[36]J. L. Simmons and Barry Winograd, *It's Happening* (Santa Barbara, Calif.: Mare-Laird Publications, 1966), p. 31.

[37]Rudd, *op. cit.,* p. 294.

[38]Alvorn, *op. cit.,* p. 128.

[39]*Ibid.,* p. 124.

[40]*Ibid.,* pp. 74-75.

[41]*Loc. cit.*

[42]Eldridge Cleaver, *Soul on Ice* (New York: McGraw-Hill, 1968).

[43]George Andrews and Simon Vinkenoog, eds., *The Book of Grass* (New York: Grove Press, 1968).

[44]George Ivanovitch Gurdjieff was a European mystic who attracted considerable attention during the 1920s with his system of teaching by which one sought new levels of experience by beginning with self-awareness and progressing ultimately to cosmic consciousness.

[45]Carlos Casteneda, *The Teachings of Don Juan* (Berkeley: University of California Press, 1968).

[46]See, especially, "Fun in Games," *Encounters* (Indianapolis:Bobbs-Merrill, 1961), and "Where the Action Is," *Interaction Ritual* (Garden City: Doubleday Anchor, 1968).

[47]Howard S. Becker, *Outsiders* (New York: The Free Press of Glencoe, 1963), pp. 41-58.

[48]Goffman, "Fun in Games," *op. cit.,* p. 33: "We find, then, *transformation rules,* in the geometrical sense of that term, these being rules, both inhibitory and facilitating, that tell us what modifications in shape will occur when an external pattern of properties is given expression inside the encounter.'"

[49]Free, *Revolution for the Hell of It* (New York: The Dial Press, Inc., 1968).

[50]*Ibid.,* p. 31.

[51]*Ibid.,* p. 59.

[52]*Ibid.,* pp. 62-63.

[53]*Ibid.,* pp. 61-62.

[54]See Alfred Schutz, "Commonsense and Scientific Interpretations of Human Action," *Collected Papers,* ed. Maurice Natanson (The Hague: Martinus Nijhoff, 1962), I, 3-47; and Harold Garfinkel, "A Conception of and Experiments with 'Trust' as a Condition of Concerted Action," in *Motivation and Social Interaction,* ed. O. J. Harvey (New York: Ronald Press, 1963), pp. 187-238.

[55]Harold Garfinkel, *Studies in Ethnomethodology* (Englewood Cliffs, N. J.: Prentice-Hall, 1967), pp. 35-75.

[56]Free, *op. cit.,* p. 20.

[57]*Ibid.,* p. 157.

[58]*Loc. cit.*

[59]*Ibid.,* p. 158.

[60]*Loc. cit.*

[61]Alvorn, *op. cit.,* pp. 127-28.

[62]Eldridge Cleaver, *op. cit.,* pp. 71-74.

[63]Alvorn, *op. cit.*, p. 48.

[64]In Bengal, "Gherao"—imprisoning an official in his office without food, water, or opportunity to leave, until he grants certain demands—is a newly favored tactic in labor agitation. *San Francisco Chronicle* (July 15, 1969), p. 30.

[65]See Sherri Cavan, *Liquor License* (Chicago: Aldine Press, 1966), pp. 10-13, 235-37. See also the chapter entitled "On the Time Track," in Lyman and Scott, *A Sociology of the Absurd* (New York: Appleton-Century-Crofts, 1970).

[66]Alvorn, *op. cit.*, p. 119.

[67]See Anatol Rapaport, *Two Person Game Theory* (Ann Arbor: University of Michigan Press, 1966), pp. 158-85.

[68]Alfred Schutz, "The Problem of Rationality in the Social World," *Collected Papers*, ed. Arvid Brodersen (The Hague: Martinus Nijhoff, 1964), II, 74.

[69]*Loc. cit.*

[70]Erving Goffman, *Stigma* (Englewood Cliffs, N. J.: Prentice-Hall, 1964), p. 111.

[71]See Marvin B. Scott and Stanford M. Lyman, "Paranoia, Homosexuality, and Game Theory," *Journal of Health and Social Behavior*, IX (September, 1968).

[72]Personal communication.

[73]Alvorn, *op. cit.*, p. 75.

[74]"Reflections on the Strike," *op. cit.*, p. 20.

[75]Alvorn, *op. cit.*, p. 75.

[76]Personal communication.

[77]See Edwin M. Lemert, "Paranoia and the Dynamics of Exclusion," *Human Deviance, Social Problems, and Social Control* (Englewood Cliffs, N. J.: Prentice-Hall, 1967), pp. 197-211.

Chapter V
Conclusions and Interpretations

Among theorists, debate rages over whether the individual and society are in conflict or coherence as socialization proceeds. There are those, on the one hand, who stress the possibilities of a creative existence in present-day society, ignoring its coercive character. On the other hand, the more radical view emphasizes the conflict between the individual and society, stressing the ensuing alienation of man.[1] The validity of the latter position is less important than the fact that a great many students share this perspective and translate it into an inability or unwillingness to identify with the positively sanctioned roles in the society.

Since stable personal identity[2] depends on identification with as well as distinctions from the social world,[3] youth find themselves launched on a search for elements and roles of identification at a time in the life cycle when the social structure ordinarily generates instability and occasional anxiety.[4] Helen Merrell Lynd voiced the feelings of a great many young people when she wrote: "It is almost impossible for an individual to develop a sure sense of himself unless he can find aspects of his social situation with which he can clearly identify. . . . Clear identifications are difficult when a country that describes itself as a nation of democracy, freedom, and peace practices ruthlessness toward powerful peoples, support of fascism to fight Communism, and atomic warfare."[5] Given the perception of such social contradictions, a psychological consequence is a search for identity.

In one sense, youth in general and students in particular are in a favorable position to experiment with identities. Adolescence in American society is an amorphous period, its rules undefined, and its incumbents regarded as persons passing through a transitional phase. Precisely because of its anomic and temporary character, this period affords youth unusual opportunities to try out personal styles and social themes. Moreover, Americans have traditionally regarded the years spent in high school and college as a moratorium on serious existence, a time in which students will be indulged in their naiveté and forgiven for their pranks. In this period of life young people may "sow wild oats," engage in a fairly wide variety of activities that are ordinarily discouraged, disapproved, or prohibited, and ignore certain norms of conduct—so long as both young people and their elders interpret these acts as unserious. Thus for many years few persons were outraged when Berkeley students burned the city streetcars as a prelude to the "Big Game" between the University of California and Stanford.[6] Similarly, fraternity boys have traditionally engaged in sadistic and homo-erotic acts in order to initiate new members without arousing community fears of a breakdown in the mores or a sexual revolution.[7] And when university students engaged in mass raids on sorority houses, disrupting study, destroying property, and demanding items of lingerie from the girls, few adults thought it was more than an unusual form of youthful exuberance. When, however, both students and the community define extra-curricular activities as political, an indulgent attitude is no longer prominent. In short, so long as students restrict their leisure-time activities to the non-serious realms of life their disruptive acts are likely to be defined as pranks and their moratorium on assuming adult roles is likely to be continued without question.

Changes in the larger social structure, however, have made this tacit social contract between youth and society very precarious. Increasingly the college student today is a chronological or functional adult.[8] Compulsory military service and a decision to go to work before entering college insures that a considerable portion of the undergraduate population will be at or over the legal age of adulthood when they enter an institution of higher learning. Further, more and more of the occupations to which college students aspire require post-graduate study leading to certification, a master's degree, or the doctorate. This means that some persons—despite their age, experience, marital status, and civic orientations—will be regarded as students until they are in their late twenties or beyond.

Today young people are simultaneously more mature and yet less autonomous because of the anachronistic structure of institutions in America. The educational system places such a significant premium on precocity that students experience their break with the sheltering family in junior high school, their experience in an adolescent subculture in the middle years of youth, and become anxiously aware of the importance of any misstep for their futures during their years in high school. Their contacts with the opposite sex occur earlier in adolescence and serious romances and marriage take place sooner than the older middle-class ideal encouraged. At the same time, if they go on to higher education and especially to post-graduate studies, these already mature students are kept in a state of enforced adolescence by the complex and variegated *in loco parentis* rules and customs that are characteristic of American colleges and universities.

One cause for the failure of college or community to give adequate recognition to the adults that make up the student body is the existence of a lingering myth supportive of industrial society, namely, that one is not an adult until one is gainfully employed and a productive member of society. By definition and by common understanding, students, regardless of age and part-time or previous employment, are not regarded to be such. Rather, they are perceived as a leisure class, especially exempted because of affluence, intelligence, or good fortune, from entering into full adult responsibilities. It is as a special group with leisure privileges that students suffer the hostility and envy of those groups not similarly situated. Like unemployed Negroes and poor people on relief, students are sometimes imagined to be enjoying a style of life to which they are not entitled.

There are reasons, then, for students to find acceptable an ideology that deprecates the social order and proclaims new identities. As Jenks and Riesman point out:

> This combination of precocity and enforced dependency encourages students to create a make-believe world in which it is "as if" they were grown up. To achieve this they must organize their own lives, define their own limits, set their own ideals, and deny the authority and legitimacy of the adult world which they cannot join.[9]

Ideology redefines the student role as that of an adult. Among other things the current ideology calls for an abrogation of the old and now anachronistic bargain by which the student moratorium on responsibility was maintained so long as students confined their disruptive activities to non-serious realms of life. Students wish to expand the definition of their status to encompass planning undergraduate and graduate curricula, hiring, promoting and retaining faculty, controlling the admission requirements of the university, and governing their own personal, sexual, and social lives. By insisting on their seriousness of purpose, by placing themselves on an equal (or even superior) status with respect to faculty and administrators, by calling for an end to the formality and etiquette that separates students from teachers, and by insisting on the abolition of all forms of dependency, students convert their adolescent status to that of an adult.

The situation is compounded and intensified by the presence and orientation of militant blacks on the campus. At the very moment when they seek to forge a new identity for themselves and their progeny—an identity that emphasizes manhood, maturity, autonomy, and an old and proud cultural heritage—the blacks find themselves to be role models for whites. Whites now see themselves as functional "niggers," deprived of their full manhood, forced into a pseudo-familistic dependency by benevolent school administrators, denied autonomy over their personal, mental, and material lives, and living out the lies of a false and hypocritical culture that denies the role of racism in its own creation. A potential conflict exists in the fact that whites seem to need "niggers" to illustrate forcefully their own sense of bondage and alienation, while blacks resent being exploited as a symbol for the "liberation" of whites. Arguments among black students and intellectuals over whether to pursue an independent or integrated route to freedom, whether to insist on black capitalism or the founding of a new socialism for all America, or whether to accept short-term gains for blacks or hold out until liberation for all deprived persons is achieved, indicate the particular form this conflict presently assumes.

The status and identity of women also deserves mention. At one time in the Abolitionist movement the fates of Negroes and women were closely linked. Both were perceived as slaves to a social and political system that defined them as inferior, incapable, and immature. Later, Gunnar Myrdal pointed out that the emancipation of women and children and the emancipation of Negroes have much in common and are closely interrelated:

> In the final analysis, women are still hindered in their competition by the function of procreation; Negroes are laboring under the yoke of the doctrine of unassimilability which has remained

although slavery is abolished. The second barrier is actually much stronger than the first in America today. But the first is more eternally inexorable.[10]

More recently Betty Friedan, in a widely read book, described the frustrations and anxieties that arise because a "feminine mystique" supports women's continued state of inequality as well as their unfulfillment as persons. "But," Miss Friedan concluded, "the time is at hand when the voices of the feminine mystique can no longer drown out the inner voice that is driving women on to become complete."[11]

Concomitant with the movement in behalf of Black Power has been a movement favoring woman power. Under the impact of recent events, sex-role specificity has broken down more and more. In the communes established in liberated buildings, insurrectionist youth push this breakdown further and further to its limits. Women are not only not called upon to attend to such female chores as cooking and cleaning, but they are specifically advised against such, unless they experience a sense of liberation through these activities. Rooms and functions for which the sexes were traditionally separated are integrated as acts of liberation, and squeamish girls are urged to give up any sex-specific inhibitions and anxieties they have. Women assume leadership and activity positions together with men; and they fight, resist, and go to jail along with the male protesters. The revolution on the campus offers a radical and practical solution to a major female identity problem in American culture, and this serves as an additional motive for women's support in the movement.

Aside from the cognitive acceptance of new identities, it is our contention that these revolt-generated identities are in themselves fun. In one sense any accepted identity may contain within it or evoke for its incumbent some sense of a non-rational highest value, a supreme "kick"—what Orrin Klapp has called the *summum bonum*, any value high enough to be taken as the center or purpose of life.[12] Modern industrial societies suffer from one supreme irony of their own successes: namely, that the conventionalized roles and positively sanctioned statuses are less and less productive of this sense of a supreme "kick" for their incumbents, and, more noticeably, for those presumably being prepared to assume them. Realizing their dysphoric content, not a few young people are refusing to embark on the well-worn paths to adult socialization, while those who occupy conventional statuses are "dropping out," retreating into ritualized roles, seeking eudaemonic adventures in their leisure hours, or trying to instill a sense of fulfilling meaningfulness into their routine performances.

To those who seek new identities to replace the moribund ones that society provides, a powerful motivation is that the identity provide that *sine qua non* for self-fulfilling happiness, an identification with something beyond oneself as presently perceived. The sought-after identity must not be a mere extension of the ongoing self but one that is both new and yet fulfilling of that unrealized sense of self that yearns after liberation, recognition, and response. Thus the new identities may draw upon the physical and natural resources of the person, and also bring into play already developed skills, so long as the total emergent thus called into existence is different from conventionalized usages and productive of that euphoric sense of true self-realization.

Moreover, the new identities are those with which one becomes spontaneously involved. The student revolutionaries are caught up and carried away by their activities, engrossed in the task of campus revolt. During the course of a demonstration, sit-in, building occupation, or police "bust," most participants are so deeply enmeshed in the ongoing event that, in Goffman's words, they find it "psychologically unnecessary to refrain from dwelling on it and psychologically unnecessary to dwell on anything else."[13] Spontaneous involvement is itself productive of an afterlife of euphoria. Typically it occurs, if it occurs at all, while playing a game, watching an exciting sporting event, engaging in animated conversation, or fighting off an attacker. In the nostalgic remembrance of their spontaneous involvements people generally recall a sense of unselfconscious involvement that stands in sharp contrast to that carried out in their everyday activities. Usually spontaneous involvement is recalled not only with pleasure, but with a longing to experience just such feelings more often, or, indeed, all the time.

The new identities generated by the campus revolt provide such self-realizing and spontaneously involving experiences. First they are often evoked out of the exigencies of the immediate situation, calling into play old skills for new purposes or offering the opportunity to see just what latent resources and hidden talents a person might have. An example is found in the activity of the architecture students in Avery Hall during the Columbia revolt:

> Like the students in Fayerweather, the occupants of Avery were primarily graduate students, and a great many of them were moderate. They favored compromise on the amnesty question but were repeatedly convinced by strike leaders to maintain a hard line. Most notable about Avery were its tunnel barricades. The architecture students, helped by their professors, it was said, had constructed them with the skill of professionals. They had

built critical stress points that would withstand the onslaught of hordes of police but would yield in seconds if altered in a particular way from the inside. The architects were sure that their barricades were impregnable.[14]

Spontaneous involvement was characteristic of the activity inside occupied buildings during the Columbia affair. The endless discussion sections that met to make decisions and realize participatory democracy infused people into the encounter with a manner quite unlike a classroom seminar or a regular political discussion. The division of labor that "naturally" sprang up created new roles and encompassed whole selves, closing off the awareness or conscious evocation of whatever other identities had once been part of the person. During the Columbia strike:

> The communal cohesiveness in the student-controlled buildings began soon after each takeover. The students who occupied Low, for example, had developed considerable *esprit de batiment* as early as Wednesday evening. During the following days they formed and joined task forces to serve the needs of the other occupants: some stood guard at points of contact with the outside, some kept up communications via phone and walkie-talkie with friendly buildings, and others—mostly girls—managed food and housekeeping details.[15]

As members become infused with the spirit of the event—i.e., spontaneously involved with each other—a visual and cognitive engrossment occurs that permits an effortless dissociation from all other activities, ordinarily deeply held beliefs, and social mores. The ease with which the members of the Columbia revolt decided to strip naked as a form of resistance illustrates this phenomenon:

> On Thursday night, when word of a possible bust arrived in Low, one demonstrator suggested that, in order to hamper the police, all the occupants remove their clothes when the police came. The proposal passed by a sizable majority, and it was suggested that with police action so close they begin practice drills immediately.[16]

The fun element in such actions is obvious. But for the students in revolt, fun has ceased to be just what one does for momentary excitement. It has become the search for identity. The adventure, as described by Simmel, was once a break from the humdrum existence, a break which allowed for idiosyncrasy, the practice of secret roles, and the realization of suppressed dreams—but it was always just an interruption, a temporary departure, a vacation from the conventional life to which the adventurer would eventually return. Now, in true dialectical fashion, those in revolt are asserting the right to have an adventurous life without having to return to routine existence. Rather than a zestful departure from ordinary life, the adventure, the kick, is to take on a dramatic "routinization" of its own. The exhilaration of the campus revolt is seen as a rehearsal and a prelude for a new life.

Identity transformation, personal discovery, and the embarkation on new roads of selfhood are not only evocative of euphoria and joy, however. Assuming these identities or even taking the first steps toward a break with conventional society makes for a life that is both more intense and more problematic. The emotional content of thrills includes both exhilaration and anxiety. Thus the pattern of retribution for campus disturbances threatens the participants' entire future. Students are liable to a multiple jeopardy of arrest and conviction, expulsion from their university, destruction of their career aspirations, and the countless ignominies that arise from having a criminal record. In many and varied ways students on college campuses are faced with the question, "What will my life be about now?" The spirit of existential *angst*—the mixture of fear, anxiety, and, most of all, uncertainty that is created in the mind by the climate of revolt and repression on the campus—is revealed in the statement by a coed:

> How I stand on the strike is how I stand in relation to the rest of society: on a tightrope. On a tightrope mechanically making my way to the other side, some goal, not knowing whether or not I want to reach the goal or to fall off the rope. To fall off the tightrope into "the" revolution, a revolution, my revolution, what revolution? What? I don't know . . . so I continue to struggle along the rope during the wind to blow me, push me, topple me into a new way of life.[17]

Those who join the revolt may suffer the anxieties that come with understanding a new, uncertain way of life, but at least some of these persons feel that exchange of the shams of routine career security for the realities of truly self-fulfilling activity is worth the cost. They have accepted the challenge to overcome their past impotence, quit the ephemeral comforts of the campus life, and finally realize the age-old dream of an actual community.[18]

Territorial
Imperatives

The quest for community is a vague abstraction in the mind-life of students. It materializes in concrete form only when translated into an active search for territorial control.

Among humans in organized activity we may distinguish free and unfree territories. The former are characterized by freedom of access and action; the latter by rules of access and activity controls. Among free territories we may distinguish personal and group types. Personal territories are characterized by their privacy and seclusion; within them a man can engage in idiosyncratic and prohibited acts. Group territories are areas where numbers of people, normally under scrutiny or authority, may engage in unsupervised activities.[19] Free territories are carved out of space by accident or design, and in addition to their opportunities for unfettered activities they are areas for the realization and maintenance of specialized identities.

Central to the manifestation of these opportunities are enclosure and the creation of boundaries. This is so because activities that run counter to expected norms require seclusion or invisibility to permit unsanctioned performance, and because peculiar identities are sometimes impossible to realize in the absence of an appropriate setting.[20] Thus the opportunities for freedom of action—especially with respect to normatively discrepant behavior and the maintenance of specific identities—are intimately connected with the ability to attach boundaries to space and command access to or exclusion from territories.

We may further distinguish four types of territorial unit according to the modes of behavior that each permits: public territories, home territories, interactional territories, and body territories.[21]

Public territories are all those areas to which an individual has freedom of access, but not necessarily of action, by virtue of his claim to general societal membership or citizenship. Home territories are public areas taken over by groups or individuals for purposes of securing special activities from intrusion or invasion. Interactional territories are areas where social gatherings take place bounded by social rules of entrance and egress. The space encompassing the human body and that area around it that is regarded as personal define the boundaries of body territory.

Much campus dispute arises over attempts to convert public to home territories. Debates over whether the crisis at Berkeley in 1964 was over freedom of speech or something else usually overlook the territorial issue. Students insisted that Sproul Hall Plaza was rightfully their own area and thus subject to rules of speech conduct formulated by themselves. The administration sought at times to prohibit and usually to regulate student conduct in that area, insisting that, as a public place, Sproul Hall Plaza was subject to just those rules of time, place, and manner that govern all such places. In the years that have followed the compromise settlement of that issue, students have marked their partial victory over the administration by decorous identity pegs signifying the special place that the plaza holds for them. Hippie clothing, partial nudity, spontaneous musical gatherings, tables distributing political literature, hawkers of food, soft drinks, and graffiti-inspired lapel buttons, religious and political demagogues, and circles of students hotly debating current, controversial issues—all these are characteristic features that set the plaza off from other places and mark it as the peculiar place established by the students for free expression.

The struggle over a people's park in Berkeley constitutes a dramatic instance of the attempt to establish a home territory. Students and their compatriots, designating themselves as the "street people" sought to colonize on a university-owned empty lot. In the absence of any activity there, they designed a makeshift park and recreation area with transplanted sod, rude benches, slides and swings, and a hastily constructed bandstand. The street people gathered at the park to play and listen to music. Some of them slept there and complaints were heard of sexual license and marijuana smoking. A confrontation of major proportions—involving use of police, highway patrolmen, national guardsmen, and dropping a powerful tear gas from helicopters—ensued when university administrators (prodded by local and state officials) insisted on enclosing the people's park behind a steel fence and enjoining its use as a recreation area for street people.

In the course of their revolt, students often create home territories out of city streets, public corridors, and private offices. The Berkeley street people have demanded in vain thus far that Telegraph Avenue, an area adjacent to the University of California, be converted to a mall where they might carry on with impunity the social and cultural activities associated with their newly asserted style of life. During the occupation of Sproul Hall by Berkeley students in 1964, free university classes were held, Jewish students celebrated Chanukah, and halls and classrooms were converted into communal settings in which the "liberated life" could be lived. During the six-day occupation of Columbia University's Low Library, the private office of President Grayson Kirk became living quarters and a revolutionary commune for almost two hundred students.

Student actions over territories are held to be unwarranted encroachments when these actions are defined as violations, invasions, and contaminations. Violations of territory include any unwarranted use of them. When students and their non-student compatriots, in defiance of rules prohibiting the use of loud speakers and other sound-amplifying instruments, call a public meeting on university property and use public address systems, they violate a territory, from an administrative viewpoint. And when armed militia and police drive street people from their established people's park, they violate a home territory. Violators are those who have repulsed or circumvented those who would deny them access. Furthermore, they are also, by virtue of their acts, claimants, in some sense, to the territory which they have violated. Their claims, however, may vary in scope, intensity and objective. Students may make unwarranted use of a classroom building only to dramatize other grievances they have against the university. On the other hand, revolutionaries may try to destroy for all time the computer equipment of a university in order to put an end to their impersonal and anonymous treatment by administrators and faculty.

Invasion of a territory occurs when those not entitled to entrance and use nevertheless cross the boundaries and interrupt, halt, take over, or change the meaning of an already defined arena of activity. Acts that if committed by a single person or a small group would be defined as a minor violation or an annoying interruption, are, if carried out by crowds, defined as invasions. Thus one student heckling an instructor, or a small group seeking confrontational audience with a dean are not generally regarded as invasions even if the behavior passes beyond the bounds of propriety. But when five hundred singing, clapping, and shouting students enter a building, drive out its regular inhabitants, take over its offices and corridors, build barricades against the police, and threaten a long-term or even permanent occupancy, an invasion has occurred.

Because of its symbolic challenge to authority, perhaps the most serious form of territorial encroachment is contamination—that is, the conversion of the sacred to the profane. In a revolution against the existing order, its sacred objects come under attack. Thus, a nation's flag is burnt and its president is hanged in effigy. Since sacred objects are often characterized by their insulation from touch, sight, or sound, one mode of profanation is contamination by exposure. In a university revolt the sacred character of a president's office is often enhanced by privileged access and special objects. In addition, the incumbent himself and his private possessions assume a sacred quality of which they can be deprived by contamination. Thus, when they invaded President Grayson Kirk's office "students toyed with office equipment, sipped Kirk's sherry and puffed his White Owl 'President' cigars."[22] Euphoric spirits prevailed because "the quarters they occupied were the *sanctum sanctorum* of Columbia University. Kirk's offices had *de facto* been off limits for students of the University, except under extraordinary circumstances."[23]

Aside from attempts at conversions of public territories—whether through contamination or some other form of encroachment—some students have attempted to transform the meaning and boundary of academic interactional territories. Surrounding every interactional territory is an invisible boundary, a kind of social membrane that segregates the human cluster that makes it up. Moreover, every interactional territory makes a claim of boundary maintenance for the duration of the interaction and against all those who are defined as unprivileged to enter its domain. Access and egress are governed by rules understood, though not necessarily promulgated, by the members.

Based on long-known status differences, a characteristic boundary and manner defines student-faculty interaction. Generally clothing style differences, style of speech, and situational segregation have marked these differences. The students in revolt seek to end this social separation and status signification. A now famous essay that has been reprinted in many campus newspapers announces that students are "niggers." As evidence of this ignominious status the author points out at "Cal State L.A. where I teach, the students have separate and unequal dining facilities." He goes on to complain that

> If I take them into the faculty dining room my colleagues get
> uncomfortable, as though there were a bad smell. If I eat in the
> student cafeteria, I become known as the educational equivalent
> of a niggerlover. In at least one building there are even rest-
> rooms which students may not use. At Cal State, also, there is
> an unwritten law barring student-faculty lovemaking. Fortu-
> nately, this anti-miscegenation law, like its Southern counterpart,
> is not 100 percent effective.[24]

In addition to demanding student-faculty integration of college cafeterias, lavatories, and sexual intercourse, there is also a strong opposition to the deference that once was regarded as the ordinary courtesy due to a professor. Redefined as the etiquette of a demanding caste system much like that of the deep South, the use of honorific titles is seen as a subtle deterrence to student freedom and equality. The critic from Cal State writes: "A student . . . is expected to know his place. He calls a faculty member 'Sir' or 'Doctor' or 'Professor'—and he smiles and shuffles some as he stands outside the professor's office."[25] As this critic sees it, the student is victimized by a hopelessly authoritarian system.

The modes by which formalism and status distinctions are broken down are many and varied. Some encourage that classroom lectures be ended and that open, free-wheeling discussions replace them; that professors drop all affectations of status and instead insist on their equality with students; and further that professors indicate this equality and informality by casual dress, colloquial speech, and after-class associations. Others wish to abolish teaching altogether, preferring to rely on "free universities" administered, taught, and tended by "learners," i.e., the students. Still others insist that teachers and administrators bare their inner lives, expose their "hang ups," and confess to their pretensions and shortcomings in therapeutic sessions conducted by faculty, students, and laymen on a "no holds barred" basis. Whatever the mode, however, the object is the abolition of all distinctions that presently differentiate student and teacher and the replacement of formality, deference, and insulation by intimacy, fraternization, and availability.

Related to the attack on status distinctions and privileged interaction is the incipient revolution in body exposure, usage, and touch relationships. The human body is the most private and inviolate of territories belonging to any individual. Rights to view and touch it are of a sacred nature and subject to many restrictions.[26] The space immediately surrounding the body is also inviolate, constituting a personal space to which entrance is normatively governed and generally restricted.[27] One element of the current revolt, however, is an assault on the privileged status of the body. Its most general form is opposition to any inhibitions concerning the body and its exposure and uses. Public nudity, a more promiscuous orientation concerning sex, and violation of the established taboos on body contact are all practiced and encouraged as signs of "liberation." Relaxation of censorship codes and a new interest in nudity and sex in drama, films, and novels—in part an effect of the new revolutionary morality—have added further legitimacy to this aspect of the current movement. Persons seeking relief from alienation, liberation from psycho-social inhibitions, or sexual freedom find outlets in the promises of sensitivity-training, the philosophy of joy through increased tactile awareness, and the pleasures obtained in therapeutic communities of unashamed and naked people.

Another function of the interested legitimacy of body contacts espoused in the movement is that of communicating and reinforcing group solidarity and commitment. The mass of students in revolt—in exception to the leaders—tend not to voice their commitments. Indeed it is their actions, not their words, that constitute a "propaganda of the deed" in support of revolutionary goals. Yet, in times of anxiety and stress, members need to feel they are not acting alone, or following a line that has little support. In the absence of clear statements of mutual commitment, members of the movement more freely touch, embrace and fondle one another, and in the process feel the physical presence and infer the social solidarity of their compatriots. Concomitant with the cramped quarters, promiscuous sex, and sharing of heretofore unshared facilities—sleeping quarters, toilets, showers—the breakdown of inhibitions concerning body territories and personal space facilitates the notion that others are equally committed to the ideology and the protest.

In sum, territorial imperatives are crucial elements in current ideology; and actions in behalf of territorial establishment and liberation constitute, at least for the moment, goals of the movement. In turn territorial control tends to insure ideological commitment, social solidarity, and moral fervor.

Interpretations

Two kinds of interpretation can be placed upon the current student movement. According to one interpretation, the movement has concrete aims, and specific means are devised for their attainment. It is organized in terms of certain intended social objectives which are well recognized by the students who plan and devise the carefully selected programs of action, and who attempt to achieve these programs at the price of sacrifice, struggle and suffering. Call this the *agony* model. On the other hand, student rebellion may be conceived as collective outbursts, whose goals are really to be understood in terms of the unintended features that emerge in the course of student activism and have their most profound effects on the participants themselves, producing a new-found sense of identity and fun. Call this the *ecstasy* model. Let us examine more closely the arguments that might be made for asserting the primacy of each of these interpretations.

the Agony Model

In the history of attacks on established authority, we may distinguish three distinct modes, delineated by escalating degrees of alienation from the given structure of authority. First, there is the approach of *reform*. According to the ideas that underlie this challenge, nothing at all is fundamentally wrong with the basic value system and little is wrong with the institutions and instrumentalities by which social change is effected. What is needed is an application of already developed and perfectly legitimate techniques to achieve agreed-upon and important ends in a sector of society that has for some reason been needlessly neglected. When the Supreme Court ruled that public schools must desegregate, it acted in a reformist tradition, despite applause or anxiety in some quarters about the "revolutionary" change that would be brought about. Similarly, when voting rights are extended to heretofore unfranchised classes of the population, when charitable aid is organized and dispensed by governmental agencies, and when established regulations affecting health, morals or safety are extended to encompass a greater institutional scope, reformist activities are underway. Reform challenges authority to apply its own recognized principles and time-tested policies to arenas of neglect, inequity, and suffering that without violating cherished values deserve positive and beneficent attention.

A greater degree of alienation from authority is exhibited in *rebellion*. Rebels typically focus on the ineptitude, impropriety, or downright evil of those who hold power, but they do not challenge the legitimacy of the authority structure as such. Rebellion traditionally has taken the form of individual or gang-organized banditry, looting, or assassination. In those societies where the official system of authority had great legitimacy among the masses—such as traditional China—rebels frequently confessed to their criminal acts and accepted capital punishment on the promise that their admittedly wrongful deeds had called attention to a social problem that would be remedied.[28] Even in those societies where bandits do not so readily give themselves up, folk-lore and popular belief enshrines them as local heroes engaged in an altogether proper redistribution of wealth or a remedy for oppression. Typically social banditry arises under conditions of stress, in areas where official authority has little popular support, and among sectors of the population not yet influenced by fully articulated ideologies.

Rebellion may take on a populist or conservative character, depending on the situation.[29] In the former instance it identifies with the local poor, assumes an unauthorized paragovernmental position in righting wrongs, dispensing justice, and donating a portion of its stolen monies to impoverished people. It even seeks to supplant local government with its own members and style. In the latter instance, local, rebellious toughs are employed or volunteer their services in support of the social order and against the rebellious populists or revolutionary organizations of other disaffected groups. In America there has been a long history of social banditry by individuals or groups in unsettled areas and in ghettos inhabited by persons culturally and socially distant from the larger society.[30] A new populism has been enunciated by black and other minorities who, under the influence of slogans like "Black Power," are demanding that local ethnic officials govern compact communities organized on racial or national lines. Thus far it has not taken on the full character of social banditry, but the concept of "liberated property" held by the Black Panthers bids fair to herald just such a phenomenon. Conservative rebellion is also emerging in America. Motorcycle gangs composed of alienated lumpenproletarians have on occasion voluntarily joined with police and other officials in attacking rebellious college students, while angry fraternity members and conservative college students have formed political clubs and "flying squads" of toughs to support college administrators and state governments in their opposition to the revolts from the left.

Beyond rebellion, with its ultimate support for the social order, is *revolution*—which seeks to destroy the social order and replace it with another built upon entirely different principles. Revolutionary behavior traditionally arises among those classes vulnerable to ideological rhetoric, radical leadership, and intellectual influence. Whereas reform seeks to extend the benevolent instrumentalities of the existing order, and rebellion seeks to harass and overthrow the unjust officials of a just society, revolution seeks neither to tinker with institutions nor tamper with officialdom. It seeks nothing less than a new order.

Whether a movement is reformist, rebellious, or revolutionary affects the pace and rhythm of its operations. A reform movement drifts forward in slow, seemingly orderly, continuous, and pragmatic steps. Rebellion operates in sporadic and intermittent uprisings—against this official and that institution—with less regard for incremental progress or clear direction. Revolution moves forward in accordance with ideologically informed strategies and ultimate goals. Now in the case of the action on campus, the shift from reform to rebellion to revolution is significant. The reformer, seeking only to remedy a bad situation says, "Let us petition the administration to end ROTC on this campus." When the administration says that it cannot simply abolish a portion of the curriculum upon a student's request, the reformer is abashed, but the rebel says, "Let us stage a demonstration, shut down a portion of the university, and dramatize our objection to militarism on campus." If the demonstration drags on, multiplies in scope and issues, and commands considerable public attention, it may inspire the revolutionary to emerge and say, "Let us expand our operations, inform ourselves of the totality of our situation, and organize not merely to end one facet of our oppressive existence, but to end oppression itself. Let us abolish the conditions that create our alienation and create a new society founded on true liberty, real equality, and sincere brotherhood." The result is a shift from the directional drifting of reform tempo to the episodic pace of rebellion and ultimately to the continuous activism of revolution.

Trying accurately to distinguish rebellious from revolutionary aims in the campus revolts is difficult because of the complex and contradictory role of deception that prevails in these situations. Revolutionary aims may be camouflaged behind rebellious or reformist rhetoric. Demands for the abolition of ROTC, the establishment of an ethnic studies program, or the right to build and occupy a "people's park"—all specific enough to be designated as reformist in nature—are also interpretable as revolutionary imperatives, the granting of which would constitute significant strides forward in the long road to social reorganization. On the other hand, revolutionary demogoguery—including such populist slogans as "all power to the people" and such deadly threats as are implied in "up against the wall, motherfucker"—might be the carefully exaggerated rhetoric of a movement that really seeks only reforms that it expects will not be granted unless a more strident and exaggerated tone is employed in the protest. Probably both reformist and revolutionary tones are employed by protesters who are themselves unclear about the extent of their demands or the depth of the disaffection from the social order. The advantage of mixed rhetorics and unclarified purposes is that of increasing the tactical flexibility of the protesters.

The student activists are caught in a dilemma over whether to admit they are rebels or revolutionaries. On the other hand, ideology dictates an insistence on candor, a return to honesty in opposition to the "hypocrisy" of the establishment, and a frank response to all issues. Slogans such as "tell it like it is," "down to the nitty-gritty," and "that's where it's at" call attention to the open-faced orientation that the movement is supposed to espouse. On the other hand, tactics employed at any time during the course of the movement may call for secret meetings, clandestine pacts, and confidential negotiations. Furthermore, deception, trickery, and fraud may become weapons in the struggle especially as each side comes more and more to distrust the other. Ideologically committed youth may find themselves caught in a terrible dilemma when they try to choose between the candor required by revolutionary ideology and the chicanery dictated by political exigency.

Despite these complexities and contradictions, the general orientation of rebels and revolutionaries converges at one point. The general level at which this convergence occurs and unites all the apparently disparate elements of protest is that of the vast metaphysical debate on the nature of man and society. More specifically, the debate concerns the role of man in changing the state of the world in which he lives. At its most philosophical level there is a vigorous debate over two modes of social change—evolutionary and revolutionary. The former refers to changes that are slow, orderly, continuous, and in accord with the general system in which they occur; the latter are rapid, fundamental, discontinuous, and in accord with a vision of an altogether new social order. One's position in this debate is in turn determinative of modes of orientation toward action, time, and the self.

Interestingly enough there is an area of agreement at the extremes of this debate which apparently both sides among the current protagonists reject. It concerns the role of man as actor and instrument. In both the ultimate version of evolutionary theory and the historical determinacy that accompanies much ideological discussion of revolutionary change, man has little to do but await the inevitable. For evolutionists, change is ordained in the nature of the thing changing, be it biological or social. A society, then, will move in accordance with the direction of its internal dynamic and at the rate dictated by the acceleration of that dynamic. Men in such a society are constrained neither to hurry the inevitable metamorphosis nor to put impediments in its progress. Rather they are advised to wait, watch, and adjust in accordance with that which must and will occur when it is supposed to. The greatest virtue here is patience; the greatest folly, a headlong attempt to halt or hasten progress.

Historical determinacy poses a similar problem. Society fluctuates according to the historical imperatives that push it toward an inevitable disintegration followed by an equally inevitable synthesis. Change is dictated by forces that are beyond the scope of individuals to modify. Men who subscribe to the ultimate dictates of historical determinism find themselves suffering the inconveniences of inevitability. On the one hand, to seek to hasten the inexorable forces of destiny might be "left wing deviationism," an attempt to produce the revolution before its appointed time. On the other hand, to capitalize on its slowness might be "right wing opportunism," an attempt to fall back at just the moment when the revolution is about to break out. Since the revolution is inevitable, of what use is any particular human action? Again, waiting appears to be wise, though painful and full of wonder and anxiety.

Somewhere between these poles of patient waiting and anxious wonder the debate is joined. Human action is important. But what kind? How much? And to what end? To the reformer, and also the rebel, the good society will be brought about by increments, each one alleviating some suffering, establishing some benefit, until the last and final vestige of oppression, injustice, and wretchedness has been eliminated. To the revolutionary, the activities of reformers and rebels are at once signs of the inevitable change and shibboleths of false hope. They herald the fall of the corrupt social order and shore up a sagging social structure that will surely crumble or explode. The same act can have a double meaning. To the reformer it can be a measure aimed at improving a good society; to a revolutionary it can be one more moment in the irrevocable time-clock of revolutionary history. Reformer, rebel, and revolutionary are joined in their diverse interpretations of the same phenomena.

It is worth noting here an irony of major proportions. Recent social commentators have suggested that the Protestant Ethic is dead in advanced industrial societies, especially America. It has been swamped by the forces of hedonism,[31] drained of all *élan* by the gnawing search for security,[32] and replaced by a slothful surfeit of leisure, unrefined by any clear ethic whatsoever.[33] Quite possibly, however, this is only true for certain sectors of the society and in relation to a highly particularistic interpretation of the Protestant Ethic which has for so long been associated with the bourgeois class that we may neglect to see a similar though secular ethic rising with its own peculiar form in other parts of society.

The Protestant Ethic referred to more than an ascetic denial of self-indulgence. According to Weber, it included the fundamental belief that man through his own efforts and God's ineluctable will could conquer and subdue the mundane world and, in the process, receive a sign of his own election in the afterlife. Thus Weber wrote: "It was through the consciousness that his conduct, at least in its fundamental character and constant ideal (*propositum oboedientiae*), rested on a power within himself working for the glory of God; that it is not only willed of God but rather done by God that he attained the highest good toward which this religion strove, the certainty of salvation."[34] The pursuit of wealth was a moral duty once the opportunity to pursue it was presented. "Wealth is thus bad ethically only in so far as it is a temptation to idleness and sinful enjoyment of life, and its acquisition is bad only when it is with the purpose of later living merrily and without care. But as a performance of duty in a calling it is not only morally permissible, but actually enjoined."[35] And finally: "With the consciousness of standing in the fullness of God's grace and being visibly blessed by Him, the bourgeois businessman, as long as he remained within the bounds of formal correctness, as long as his moral conduct was spotless and the use to which he put his wealth was not objectionable, *could follow his pecuniary interests as he would* and feel that he was fulfilling a duty in doing so."[36]

When we consider the general conditions under which the Protestant Ethic invoked the spirit of capitalism, we come closer to understanding the modern parallel in the current revolt. The Calvinist conception of life and afterlife revealed a heretofore unrecognized God, who rules the universe arbitrarily and without counsel, advice, or even a sympathetic ear to the pleas and prayers of those over whom He exercised His majestic authority. The world was thus rendered meaningless as far as man's faculties were concerned since none could know God's divine purposes nor fathom the plan behind His holy reasoning. The Puritan response to this was neither fatalistic resignation, despairing suicide, nor a rush into headlong hedonism, but rather an activation of the human spirit in search of that which the inscrutable deity had decreed. Calvinists set out to uncover the awful truth of their own election or damnation; they restlessly sought signs and indications of that over which they had no control whatsoever. In its most general terms, then, Weber suggested that when the world reveals its meaninglessness in utterly unambiguous terms, the men who realize that awful truth plunge into courses of action, undertake new and enormous risks, seek out opportunities for their talents, and enter into a world of unpredictable outcomes all of which create meaning out of the void whose discovery originally set them in motion. As Weber put it: "For when asceticism was carried out of the monastic cells into everyday life, and began to dominate worldly morality, it did its part in building the tremendous cosmos of the modern economic order."[37]

In the current situation we hold that a similar though secular transformation is taking place. No longer concerned with an afterlife, man is perforce pushed back into fundamental concern with the mundane world and its meaning. One solution to the problem of meaning has been order and the routinization of activity in institutions. These institutions take on a character that is sacred though the commitment to institutionalized behavior ordinarily goes on unrecognized, existing at the subliminal level of cognition. So long as everyone goes about his affairs without challenging the subterranean social contract whose threads of custom and routine weave together the social order, man is content with his existence or made restless only by intra-societal frustrations.

But the current revolutionaries have carried their argument to the most fundamental area of social order. They have asserted the final break with order itself by seeking to separate function from form, process from mold, and living from life. They revolt ultimately in the name of pure activity absolutely separating that activity from any form or institution with which it might be associated. Since the forms of life, the institutions of mankind, the modes of behavior are what lend meaning to existence, this challenge, like that of Calvin's terrible discovery of God's unknowable potency, renders the world meaningless. The recipes for living that lay securely below the consciousness of man are now forcibly raised up to awareness and scrutiny, and their efficacy, value, and meaning are perceived as unknown, improbable, or unsure. In the face of this frightening revelation, some men throw themselves into frantic search for pleasure; others retreat into slavish servitude to mindless activities; others seek to form new institutions that will provide identity and security; still others resist the recognition of what the revelation shows; and, finally, some plunge into action, ride out in a bold challenge to an uncertain fate, accept the gauntlet flung down by an inscrutable *fortuna* and seek to overcome her with their own *virtu*. The revolutionaries on the campus number among them the modern equivalent of the once daring though ascetic Puritans. And out of their mystifying actions may come yet a new cosmos.

Those who see in the student revolt a movement directed toward the attainment of specific social goals focus on its vision of a new society that is organized in accordance with values radically different from presently held principles, or in its reformist-rebellious orientation toward specific social ills of the current social order. In either case it is important to note that the students appear to be more inspired by what Weber called *Wertrationalitat* rather than by *Zweckrationalitat*.[38] The former term refers to an orientation toward the achievement of a single end or a set of related ends that is so zealous as to take no account of the relationship that might exist between the objectives sought and other objectives, nor to weigh the "costs" of the means chosen with respect to other consequences that might flow therefrom. *Zweckrationalitat*, on the other hand, is an orientation toward action that considers the particular objective sought in terms of a plurality of related ends and counts the cost with respect to means in terms of possible undesirable consequences. *Wertrationalitat* is an orientation that flows from the sense of righteousness that encloses those seeking social change. The youthful students' righteousness is inspired in part by their own innocence, an innocence born of the fact that the very conditions of life against which they revolt are the products of decisions over which they have no control. If the society is in fact ruled by a "military-industrial complex," if human success is limited by the machinations of the "white power structure," and if the university is

an abject tool of the establishment, then young people can insist
that they are angrily responding to a world which is not of their own
making, and, therefore, one for which they need feel no responsibility.
Mark Rudd summed up the spirit of a visionary future achieved
through *Wertrationalitat* when he wrote the following to President
Grayson Kirk:

> We do have a vision of the way things could be: how the
> tremendous resources of our economy could be used to eliminate
> want, how people in other countries could be free from your
> domination, how a university could produce knowledge for
> progress, not waste consumption and destruction . . . how men
> could be free to keep what they produce, to enjoy peaceful lives,
> to create. These are positive values, but since they mean the
> destruction of our order, you call them "nihilism." In the move-
> ment we are beginning to call this vision "socialism." It is a fine
> and honorable name, one which implies absolute opposition to
> your corporate capitalism and your government; it will soon be
> caught up by other young people who want to exert control over
> their own lives and their society.
>
> You are quite right in feeling that the situation is "potentially
> dangerous." For if we win, we will take control of your world,
> your corporation, your University and attempt to mold a world
> in which we and other people can live as human beings. Your
> power is directly threatened, since we will have to destroy that
> power before we take over. . . . We will have to destroy at
> times, even violently, in order to end your power and your sys-
> tem—but this is a far cry from nihilism. . . .
>
> There is only one thing left to say. It may sound nihilistic to
> you, since it is the opening shot in a war of liberation. I'll use
> the words of LeRoi Jones. . . : "Up against the wall, mother-
> fucker, this is a stick-up."[39]

the Ecstasy Model

The events of the student revolt and their meaning to those who
participate permit a second and fundamentally different interpretation
than that suggested by the agony model. According to this second view
the revolt is concerned less with the achievement of concrete external
aims than with the evocation of feeling and the establishment of
identity.

Much of the current revolt takes concrete form in rallies, riots,
demonstrations, strikes, and prolonged sit-ins—in other words, in col-
lectivities informed by a high degree of consensus, contagion, and

ecstasy.[40] In one sense these expressive crowds afford precisely that concrete situation by which social solidarity is created, affirmed, and maintained. The solidarity involves the welding together of heretofore non-solitary entities of individuals, aggregates, and specific groups. For some, this solidarity is itself a goal, and one which is not realized in action directed externally but rather in the change exerted on individual internal states of consciousness and feeling. And for those who take the change in internal states seriously, it is precisely such metamorphoses as these that do exert a change in the social and institutional world.[41]

The solidarity created is one that requires the surrender of individuality and the fusion of the self with the collectivity producing a new emergent, group consciousness, empowered by its strength of numbers and informed by its singleness of identity. In such acts of expressive group creation, alienation is overcome in several of its senses. First, the sense of lonely isolation vanishes as one is swept up and into a corps of compatriots who signify by sign and gesture that they are all united in identity, feeling, and purpose. Second, the feeling of impotence is destroyed by the surging sense of power that arises in the collectivity, a sense that finds form in the feelings that with such unity of purpose and *esprit de corps* anything can be accomplished. Third, meaninglessness, that gnawing sense of confusion about the world and events, is exchanged for the shared definitions of self and situation that arise in collective settings. Fourth, anomie, that sense that there are no effective and appropriate norms of conduct to regulate human affairs, vanishes in the increasing depth of trust and dependence that arises among those sharing a common intense experience. Finally, individuals lose that sense of self-estrangement, that dreaded condition in which one experiences himself as an alien, as they forge new selves, practice innovative roles, and discover "true" identities.

The "identity" function of the current revolt is one of its most significant features. In its most general sense, this identity is associated with the notion of an under-thirty generation. Such a group identity cannot be realized in isolation. To be a member of a group (not an aggregate) of youth, one needs the dramatic presentation and affirmation of this identity. Such is found in the crowds that gather in college plazas, shouting, chanting, and singing in unison, locking arms in a great physical gesture of solidarity, and marching into a building or off to a confrontation in a visible testimony to their consciousness of kind. Moreover, collective identities are realized through the media of artifacts and symbols that dramatically signify and picturesquely portray them. Among the current youth, dress, body adornment, and language serve to designate those who have joined the revolt and to set them apart from those who are supporters of the existing social order. Long hair, side burns, and clothes that give off the effect of a careless disregard for the canons of polite society are *de rigeur* for campus revolutionaries and their sympathizers. Bizarre costumes and the routine employment of obscene language in public places also serve to facilitate the "liberated" identity. But these symbols cannot be effective in isolation; hence the establishment of territorial enclaves and collective representations where the meanings of these symbols are both personally felt and socially communicated. Telegraph Avenue in Berkeley and the Haight-Ashbury in San Francisco are but two places in which symbols signify the new society.

Other identities also require a collective and dramatic presentation in order to be experienced. A youthful Mexican-American and another of Filipino extraction cannot readily realize their common membership in the "Third World" without the existence and activities of the Third World Liberation Front. A Negro cannot convert his identity to that of a black too easily in the absence of "soul brothers," Afro-American hair styles, and the wearing of daishikis. And the woman weary of her sex-role inferiority cannot experience woman power without a dramatic refusal to do "women's work," an active assertion of her equality to men, and a visible opportunity to display talents and skills supposedly lodged solely in the opposite sex. Identity transformation requires comrades who become the convert's new reference group and ceremonies in which the new identity is experienced and affirmed. The campus demonstrations are just such occasions for identity conversion and personal self-realization.

If one observes these demonstrations on a day-to-day basis, one witnesses a collective catharsis, a purging of guilt, shame, and anxiety, and a gargantuan expression of feeling and euphoria. There seem to be endless processions, chants, songs, and shouts. At rallies, speaker after speaker begins his impromptu oration with the rhetorical question: "Why are we here?" At the opening sessions of ethnic studies classes, the instructor, drawn from the ranks of the students or from the ethnic community under discussion, frequently introduces himself with his name and the statement, "I'm seeking my identity." Shouts from the crowd—"right on, brother," "that's where it's at"—increase the enthusiasm of the speaker which, in turn, reacts back on the audience which again reciprocates escalating the excitement and spreading the contagion. The speakers do not supply new information or better arguments. Rather they provide a dramatic performance, affirming what everyone feels and translating these deep and thrilling emotions into words and phrases.

The demonstrations are public dramas that rival those of Sophocles and the other ancient Greek playwrights. With the university plaza and buildings as their stage, student protests assume the proportions of the spectacles that enthralled Attic audiences. However, the plot lines are no longer those of classical Aristotelian drama, but rather more closely resemble the Theater of the Absurd. In their forcing of public issues, employment of confrontational techniques of debate, and assumption of postures that are brazen, ludicrous, or outrageous, the demonstrations permit their participants to see how much the contemporary world is devoid of human purpose, how little mundane activities actually mean, and how deep the sensibilities are penetrated by the mere shibboleths of moral values. By reducing the everyday world of their opponents to the absurd level, the students stir interest in the recovery of man's metaphysical and transcendental roots, roots that have been buried beneath the twin idols of technical progress and human retrogression erected by twentieth-century men. In the end, the dramatic ceremonies promise relief from that kind of absurdity referred to by Camus:[42] in the new sociey a lasting marriage will be solemnized between man and his life, and the actor and his setting. The illusions of which he has been deprived will be replaced by a reality in which he can delight. The lost memories of a homeland and the false promise of a new Zion will both give way in the presence of that true *Gemeinschaft* that encompasses the entire world.

Toward
a Synthesis

According to one interpretation, the student revolt is instrumental and goal-oriented; according to another, it is expressive and fun-oriented. Which one of these interpretations is correct? Do the facts warrant a greater reliance on the agony rather than the ecstasy model? Throughout this study we have tried to show that both interpretations are correct, though each is incomplete without the other. Agony and ecstasy weave in and out of one another, sometimes one, sometimes the other assuming primacy—most often the respective emphases finding expression in discrete segments of the disenchanted student body.

There are real issues and specific goals animating the youth in revolt. In its most general sense, the revolt is against the oligarchical elites—military, industrial, political, scientific, and educational—that rule over American society and seek to dominate the world. Their values, emphasizing conformity, patriotism, and public puritanism, are rejected and in their place the students urge libertarianism, social beneficence, and honest sexuality. More specifically, the students are opposed to the Vietnam war and all its ancillary effects including heightened militarism, compulsory military service, the research on and development of atomic, biological, and chemical weapons, and the erosion of political dissent; the industrial and corporate organization of work with its emphasis on profits, teamwork, and impersonality; the political world of powerful officials, influence peddlers, republican rather than democratic representation, and the separation of the making of decisions from those affected by them; the subordination of science to both military and industrial interests coupled with an enormous emphasis on technique and the neglect of theory; and finally, the multiversity, a concept of education that suborns knowledge, wisdom and intellectual freedom to the needs of the elite who rule over an unchanging order. Crosscutting the entire structure is institutional racism, fostered by slavery and prejudice and frozen in the mindless rules, regulations, and codes of conduct and control that maintain an abject citizenry in a state of depressing debilitation. In the campus disturbances, reformers and rebels seek an end to the particular evils that a good society has spawned through ignorance and the empowering of bad officials; revolutionaries seek to destroy the fundamental social order from which all these particular evils spring and to which they are inexorably attached.

Expressive interests are also found in the student revolt. In its most general form, the youth in revolt seek to abolish alienation—that complex sense of impotence, meaninglessness, anomie, social isolation, and personal estrangement that characterizes their own lives and, so they learn, the lives of their elders as well. The revolt-in-action establishes power, generates meaning, produces norms, abolishes isolation, and creates new and fulfilling identities. Above all, the revolt creates and gives feeling to life—it provides euphoria, thrills, and fun. The spontaneous unreflective involvement in intense, ecstatic, and dangerous acts restores the lost sense of zest that the full life once had and always promises. The compact solidary units of revolt—student groups acting in conscious disregard of the divisive elements of their individual backgrounds—create an exhilarating and fulfilling experience that stands in sharp contrast to the isolated and estranged modes of existence in everyday life.

Both kinds of action—agony-generated and ecstasy-generated—require some kind of legitimation. The actual deeds that comprise the campus revolt are in violation of codes of student conduct or of public law, and, in spite of the sense of righteousness or self-fulfillment that characterizes their perpetrators, they must be justified. The ideology is the aegis under which both agony-generated and ecstasy-generated actions receive their legitimation. It is for this reason that we feel that a key feature of the student movement is the ideology of revolt.

The ideology of the current revolt, although it employs the language of earlier ideologies—especially Marxism—is not in fact one more extension of these older rhetorics of revolution. Rather it is a dramatic and "populist" extension of a cultural revolution that had its beginnings in art, philosophy, and music at the beginning of the twentieth century, but is only now realizing its potential for mass action. The distinguishing feature of this ideology, one that sets it apart from and beyond those ideologies that battled over restructuring the mundane world, is its celebration of *life itself irrespective of all forms of life*. All previous ideologies insisted on the exchange of one form of social organization and its concomitant values for yet another one, supported by new values. In this ideology, however, no new form of life is celebrated in unambiguous terms; rather, life itself—pulsating, rhythmic, spontaneous —will be liberated from all institutional bonds and act for itself. This ideology seeks to break off the continuous lineal extension of history that connects generation to generation, asserts the God-like possibilities of man to attain anything, and enunciates a formless aesthetic ethic.

The new ideology attempts a synthesis of archaic and modern senses of time and history. Its "archaic" elements are exhibited in its attempt to separate in an absolute sense this generation and all future generations from the past and its heritage. Primitive men insisted by periodic rites and ceremonies on their right and ability to abolish history and renew life from the beginning, so to speak, in a free and virginal state. The current youth in revolt assert a similar right.

The modern sense of time has rejected the primitive notion of cycles and separations from the past and substituted in its stead a linear continuum connecting a past that is irremediable to a future that is both unknown and unknowable. History for such a conception of time might be planned, perhaps, by a God for whom anything is possible. The secular youth of today have rejected the terror of this dreary continuum, and have dialectically reversed man's relation to history. For them David Rousset's existential theme, "Normal men do not know that everything is possible," is a truth. The world is transformed from its journey to an unknowable predestination into a possibilist world open to the dreams, plans, skills and opportunities of those who would dare to realize them. Thus, the ideology liberates youth from the shame and guilt of the past by severance, at the same time that it removes the future from the terrifying domination of fate and places it in their own hands.

Such an ideology justifies both agony-generated and ecstasy-generated goals. The past must be abolished, and the present-day institutions, consequences of that rejectable and rejected past, must be eliminated as well. The attacks on military adventures, compulsory service in the armed forces, deadening drudgery in corporations, and irrelevant education in the schools are all modes of cutting off one's connection to history and its evils. Moreover, since this history is one of forms, rejection of it constitutes an affirmation of life. Life itself can be fully affirmed by a concentration on acts of living, self-expression, and group identity. The formless is realized in the spontaneous acting out of life, war, and politics. The person, open to all possibilities that a limitless future offers, appears only in the freedom from restraint by all modes of life's organization. The future dissolves into an endless and spontaneous present as life acts, for the first time, in its own behalf.

Notes

[1]See Herbert Marcuse, *Eros and Civilization* (Boston: Beacon Press, 1955), pp. 101, 117, 153n. See also the discussion in Helen Merrell Lynd, *On Shame and the Search for Identity* (New York: Science Editions, 1958), pp. 183-258.

[2]For an excellent discussion of personal identity see Erving Goffman, *Stigma* (Englewood Cliffs, N. J.: Prentice-Hall, 1964), pp. 51-62.

[3]See George J. McCall and J. L. Simmons, *Identities and Interactions* (New York: The Free Press of Glencoe, 1966), pp. 63-104.

[4]See Erik H. Erikson, "The Problem of Ego Identity," *Identity and the Life Cycle*, Monograph No. 1 in *Psychological Issues* (New York: International Universities Press, 1959), pp. 101-64.

[5]Lynd, *op. cit.*, p. 215.

[6]See Max Heirich, "Demonstrations at Berkeley, 1964-65" (Doctoral dissertation, University of California, Berkeley, 1966), pp. 5-6.

[7]See Lionel Tiger, *Men in Groups* (New York: Random House, 1969), pp. 145-47.

[8]See Christopher Jencks and David Riesman, *The Academic Revolution* (Garden City: Doubleday and Co., 1968), pp. 28-50.

[9]*Ibid.*, p. 43.

[10]Gunnar Myrdal, *An American Dilemma* (New York: Harper & Bros., 1944), p. 1078.

[11]Betty Friedan, *The Feminine Mystique* (New York: Dell, 1964), p. 364.

[12]Orrin Klapp, *Collective Search for Identity* (New York: Holt, Rinehart, and Winston, 1969), pp. ix, xii.

[13]Goffman, "Fun in Games," *Encounters* (Indianapolis: Bobbs-Merrill, 1961), p. 38.

[14]Alvorn, *Up Against the Ivy Wall* (New York: Atheneum, 1968), p. 125.

[15]*Ibid.*, p. 118.

[16]*Loc. cit.*

[17]"Reflections on the Strike," *California Monthly*, LXXIX (April-May, 1969), 18.

[18]See, for example, Joseph Paff, et al., "The Student Riots at Berkeley," in *The New Student Left*, eds. Mitchell Cohen and Dennis Hale (Boston: Beacon Press, 1966), p. 253.

[19]See Erving Goffman, *Asylums* (Garden City: Doubleday Anchor, 1961), pp. 227-48.

[20]See Erving Goffman, *The Presentation of Self in Everyday Life* (Garden City: Doubleday Anchor, 1959), pp. 22-30.

[21]For an extended discussion, see Lyman and Scott, "Territoriality," *Social Problems*, XV (Fall, 1967), 236-49.

[22]Alvorn, *op. cit.*, p. 64.

[23]*Ibid.*, pp. 118-19.

[24]Jerry Farber, "The Student as Nigger," in *The Hippie Papers* (New York: Signet Books, 1968), p. 161.

[25]*Loc. cit.*

[26]For an excellent discussion, see Paul Schilder, *The Image and Appearance of the Human Body* (New York: Science Editions, 1964).

[27]See Robert Sommer, *Personal Space* (Englewood Cliffs, N. J.: Prentice-Hall, 1969), pp. 26-38.

[28]See E. J. Hobsbawm, *Social Bandits and Primitive Rebels* (Glencoe: The Free Press, 1959), pp. 1-29.

[29]See Reinhard Bendix, "The Lower Classes and the 'Democratic Revolution,'" *Industrial Relations*, I (October, 1961), 91-116.

[30]See Richard Maxwell Brown, "Historical Patterns of Violence in America," and Joe B. Frantz, "The Frontier Tradition: An Invitation to Violence," both in *The History of American Violence, op. cit.*, pp. 45-83, 127-53.

[31]See Jessie Bernard, "The Eudaemonists," in *Why Man Takes Chances*, ed. S. Z. Klausner (Garden City: Doubleday Anchor, 1968), pp. 32-34.

[32]See William H. Whyte, Jr., *The Organization Man* (Garden City: Doubleday Anchor, 1956), pp. 16-24.

[33]See David Riesman, "Work and Leisure: Fusion or Polarity?"; "Leisure and Work in Postindustrial Society"; and "Some Issues in the Future of Leisure," all in *Abundance for What?* (Garden City: Doubleday and Co., 1964), pp. 147-61, 162-83, 184-95.

[34]Max Weber, *The Protestant Ethic and the Spirit of Capitalism* (New York: Charles Scribner, 1930), pp. 114-15.

[35]*Ibid.*, p. 163.

[36]*Ibid.*, pp. 176-77. Emphasis supplied.

[37]*Loc. cit.*

[38]Max Weber, *The Theory of Social and Economic Organization*, ed. T. Parsons (Glencoe: The Free Press, 1947), pp. 115-18.

[39]Alvorn, *op. cit.*, pp. 26-27.

[40]See Herbert Blumer, "Collective Behavior," in *New Outline in the Principles of Sociology*, ed. Alfred McClung Lee (New York: Barnes and Noble, 1946), pp. 182-85.

[41]See Talcott Parsons, *The Social System* (Glencoe: The Free Press, 1951), p. 49.

[42]See the discussion in Martin Esslin, *Theater of the Absurd* (Garden City: Doubleday Anchor, 1961), pp. xix-xxi.